"In a world that is complicated and divided, we desperately need biblical answers to our honest, real-life questions. Christians need insight for how to help people understand truth in our ever more pluralistic society. Ludington's book helps us see how Romans has effectively given us what we need. This will be an incredibly helpful and timely resource for people who desire to follow Jesus in an age when everything is in question."

—**John Alwood**,
Founder & Apostolic Team Leader for
the Gospel Ventures Network

"Where do people go to get straight answers in a confusing and bent culture that often offers only dishonest or politically-correct responses? You will find real answers in *Frustrated*. With integrity and boldness, Ludington speaks with the conviction and tenderness of a pastor who has not forgotten his own brokenness. He has personally experienced grace and has found the truth."

—**Bruce Bugbee**,
Author of *What You Do Best*, *Network*
(winner of the Gold Medallion Award),
and other titles, with two million readers worldwide,
www.brucebugbee.com

"In this journey though the core themes of the book of Romans, Pastor Jeff Ludington has captured the heartbeat of Jesus. Jeff looks deeply at the truth of Scripture and then helps us see that grace sets us free to follow God and live in powerful new ways that reflect the very love and presence of Jesus. I have the privilege of knowing Jeff as a local church pastor and as a friend, and I continue to see him live a life of natural outreach that inspires me to share God's love with greater passion and grace. When Jeff writes about life, the gospel, and loving people who are far from God, I pay attention. I commend his work to you and pray that this journey through the powerful truths of the Book of Romans will not only inspire you, but will propel you into your world with the hope and good news of the Savior."

—**Rev. Dr. Kevin G. Harney,**
Founder of Organic Outreach International;
Lead Pastor of Shoreline Community Church,
Monterey, California;
author of the *Organic Outreach* trilogy of books

FRUSTRATED

HOW
THE BIBLE
RESOLVES
LIFE'S
TOUGH
QUESTIONS

JEFF LUDINGTON

LUCIDBOOKS

To Lisa, who encouraged me to write

To Generations Church, who walked this journey with me

To Jesus, for without Him, there is no story

TABLE OF CONTENTS

FOREWORD

We've all had passionate arguments with people over issues we care deeply about. In fact, the more we care about a subject, the more passionate we become, especially when the one we are arguing with cannot see what is so clear to us. We don't want to come across as arrogant, as though we know it all, which we clearly do not; but we desperately want the one we are debating to have his or her eyes opened to experience the benefit of our perspective.

I had such an argument with my wife over a major financial decision years ago. I wanted to sell our house, take the equity, and build another one. She simply did not see the pure genius of my financial plan, which was so plain to see. Instead, she was looking out for our three small children and wanted to keep a "stable home" for them. Whatever! We were both passionate about our perspectives, and we argued for weeks. It was frustrating for both of us, but in the end, the right solution for our family emerged through the struggle. Needless to say, we have a stable home.

Such is the debate in the Christian Church. There are always disagreements over countless minor areas of theology and methodology, but there is currently a growing divide

ix

within Christendom over the very foundation of our faith, including the core gospel message, how we read our Bibles, and the vision of Christian living.

This is nothing new. The Church has been debating its core message and its methodology for 2,000 years, and today is no different. From the Council at Jerusalem in 50 AD debating the many cultural complexities of Jews and Gentiles in the Church, to the present debates—including the interpretation of Scripture, the nature of the gospel, and human sexuality— the Church culture is one of constant dialog.

There are those who consider a culture of debate a sign of fragility, but I believe it is, in fact, a sign of strength. Throughout history, God's Spirit has moved through the dynamics and drama that unfold through never-ending debate within ever-changing cultures, and the Church is stronger as a result. Through the churn of debate—as frustrating as it may be at times—the brittle and temporal chaff blows away and the life-giving truth remains. The timeless and changeless gospel endures and grows deeper roots by God's providential grace within a culture of spirited dialog guided by God's Spirit.

Frustrated is an important contribution to the current debates in Christ's Church. Jeff uses the book of Romans as a steady guide to lead us through the core message of the gospel, which is the power to unite us to God by grace through faith in Christ, and the power to transform us more and more in to the image of Christ. Jeff masterfully weaves the gospel message in with his own incredible story along with stories from his many years of pastoral ministry. *Frustrated* is a transformative journey through the truths of God's word put to work in the context of our culture, our questions, and the current debates raging in the Church. The book boldly tackles the great issues of our time in a way that is filled with truth and grace, which should be the goal of all who wish to represent Jesus Christ well in our lives and ministries.

If you are a pastor, this book will provide a well organized, grace-based, and thoroughly biblical journey through the tough questions that face Christian leadership today. Jeff's approach is easily transferable to equip your leadership teams or incorporate in your teaching ministry.

If you are a volunteer leader in the church, this book will provide language you can use with everyday people struggling with everyday questions of life and faith. Your ministry will be enriched, and you will be further equipped for the work God has called you to.

If you are a follower of Christ, eager to grow, this book will provide encouragement in your faith and a solid grounding in the gospel applied in today's context.

If you are seeking truth and exploring whether the Christian faith offers satisfying answers to your questions, this book will provide a reasonable, cogent, and practical journey, discovering the historic Christian faith within the framework of the important discussions of our time.

Jeff is a friend and partner in ministry. I have seen his commitment to love the Lord with all his heart, soul, and mind, and to live out this love to his wife Lisa and to the ministry he serves. Jeff's personal story of transformation by the power of the gospel is inspiring and an example of God's grace in action. Jeff is the real deal, and his commitment to God's Word and the expression of the gospel to a lost and broken world is as authentic as it comes. *Frustrated* comes from Jeff's passion for the truth of the gospel and his passion to see the truth transform lives and transform the world.

Frustrated is a must read for anyone interested and engaged in the important questions of faith and culture. This book will help you explore, articulate, and defend the gospel to a world in desperate need of God's transforming grace through Jesus Christ.

—**Scott Treadway**
Lead Pastor/President, Rancho Church and Christian Schools;
President, California Classis, Reformed Church in America

INTRODUCTION

Why am I so frustrated?

The content of this book was originally a sermon series I taught following Easter 2016. It was designed to intrigue the guest on Easter, who may never have stepped foot in a church before. I am most strategic on days like Easter Sunday because there are always more first-time attenders then than on any other Sunday. I know that there will be some people whom I might never get to see again, so I do my best to plan well for my next message series. I always want Easter to proclaim Jesus who lived, died, and rose from the dead—the greatest miracle ever. But the next sermon series following Easter needs to be intriguing enough for the un-churched guest to want to return and hear more. Jesus came because of His overwhelming love for a broken and lost humanity, and I want to do my best to share this with as many people as possible.

Why the title *Frustrated*? As a pastor, I get frustrated about a lot of things. The church is polarized. The Bible is often seen as irrelevant—not only in the public square, but in seminaries and churches too. I'm also frustrated by the low opinion of the

1

Church in American culture. But here's where my frustration comes to a head. Often non-Christians are looking for answers to their tough questions; but instead of answers, they get polarization among Christians on social media—especially when it comes to social and political dialogue. It breaks my heart when I hear that unbelievers have tough questions about life and faith but end up frustrated themselves. Often those who are curious can't seem to find satisfying answers. Experiencing the feeling of frustration doesn't always have to be bad though. If we allow it, frustration can cause us to ask different questions and seek deeper answers.

I know what it means to struggle with these kinds of questions, and I am grateful to have found in the Bible a source of answers that satisfy and comfort me. Some people are not so fortunate and end up feeling frustrated by the seeming lack of answers. I believe God's eternal truth in the Bible is always relevant and timely. It's my hope we can find some answers together in this book.

To give some more context, these chapter title questions came from several sources. Some came from conversations I have had while counseling, and some came by following others on social media. Some came from challenging discourse with family and friends—many of whom are not Christians, several of whom are antagonistic to Christianity. What each question has in common is the need to find spiritual answers to common questions. I'll tackle questions like, "Is Loving Jesus Enough?" In our day and age, it's common for people to define their own definition of spirituality. When it comes to faith in Jesus and being a Christian, is it enough to say, "I love Jesus," or is there more to it? I'll also address the questions, "Are all sins equal, or does God treat one sin as greater than another," "Are some people more guilty than others in God's eyes?" In addition, I'll pose the questions, "Are All Christians Hypocrites," "What Is Tolerance," "What Is Judgment?" and many more.

To address these questions, I worked through passages in the Bible. What I have found over and over is that some things never change; the Bible is still relevant to us today. For this series I used the letter to the Romans so that we could develop the themes of that author. The Book of Romans was written by one of the most prominent church leaders of the first century, St. Paul the Apostle. His writing to the church in Rome deals with things we can relate to, and Roman culture was in many ways like Western American culture today.

This is also how I teach in the church I am privileged to lead. I primarily teach through books of the Bible, jumping back and forth between the New and Old Testaments. If you are not familiar, the Old Testament books were written before Jesus bodily entered into human history. The content of New Testament books address Jesus's life, death, and resurrection. Some of these New Testament books are letters from Christ-followers who saw the resurrected Jesus firsthand; these leaders helped spread the early church to the ends of the developed world.

It is my style to teach through a passage of Scripture on Sundays at Generations Church. Because of that, this book will read the same way. I will quote verses directly from the English Standard Version of the Bible, and work through each passage. Because this is a focused book aimed at answering questions, I won't always deal with detailed nuances of particular verses, and I don't cover the entire book of Romans. I will instead stay focused on the task at hand. You can always go to YouTube and watch the messages I did on those Sundays and get more textual content.

Last, why me? Why am I the one to write this book? I think the simple answer is that, in my past, I ran far from God, but He brought me back. Now I'm in a time of life when I hardly remember what it was like to be the "old me." I thank God for that, and I want others to experience what I have.

Nothing in this book is new revelation from God or even theologically profound in its own right. These are things that many have understood for a long time. But somehow this understanding has gotten lost amid the polarization within the church and our culture. Again, there is my frustration!

As you read, I pray that God will bless you with answers to your questions about the Christian faith. If you are not a follower of Jesus, my prayer is that this book shows you a Savior worthy of your heartfelt worship. I do not have all the answers, but the God who created the universe does. I am more than willing to seek the Scriptures together with you and look for the answers to our tough questions.

May you find grace and peace in the following pages.

IS LOVING JESUS ENOUGH?

Romans 1:1-17

In our day and age, it's common for people to define their own definition of spirituality. When it comes to faith in Jesus and being a Christian, is it enough to say, "I love Jesus," or is there more to it?

I met my wife Lisa when we were in grade school. I was 11 years old. When we were kids, we had a certain kind of friendship defined by life on the playground. Years later we dated in high school, and our relationship grew into something more. Eventually we committed to one another and got married. When I told Lisa I loved her, it meant I was committed to her alone. Did I need to do anything more than love her? In a sense, no. But when we got married, there were new expectations on our relationship. When I say I love Lisa, it also means I treat her well. It doesn't just mean I only have feelings for her. My love also involves real life actions. Like the saying goes, "Love is a verb." Love responds in action. When my relationship to Lisa changed and we became more committed to each other, my life reflected that change in my actions toward her. In the same way, loving Jesus has implications on my life too. What does it mean if someone says, "I'm a Christian and I love Jesus"? In one sense, "loving Jesus" is enough, but the love of Jesus moves us into action, and the apostle Paul is a key example of this.

Paul's Background before Jesus

The Apostle Paul, the author of Romans who had once been a persecutor of Christians and the Church, was confronted by the resurrected Jesus, and his life was forever changed. In Acts 9, the Bible tells us about the story of Paul's conversion on the Damascus road. Paul (then Saul) had been a religious, overzealous Jew persecuting Christians and overseeing their arrests, possibly even the tortures and executions of Christians (see Acts 7). He would kill for the sake of his faith, believing it to be pleasing to God—reflecting the mindset of what we would today call terrorism. Jesus confronted Paul—the same Jesus who had lived and been executed on the cross, and who had resurrected from death. When Paul was on the road to Damascus on his way to hassle Christians, Jesus spoke to him audibly and Saul was changed forever.

Imagine your world getting flipped upside down. Imagine that everything you once believed about God, this world, or your faith being so upended that you don't even know how to get back to where you need to be. Because of how far off Paul was and the grace Jesus showed him to bring him back, Paul would forever be indebted as a bond servant (Greek: doulos) of Christ.

Through that transformation and by understanding and

falling in love with the living Jesus, Paul found his life radically changed. Paul would go on to start many of the first-century churches, coach their leaders, and write letters to many of them. In fact, his collection of letters form about half of the New Testament writings, all addressed to different churches in different settings. His letter to the church in Rome basically says, *I long to come and see you, but until I can get there, let me help ground you in your faith. Let me help you understand what it means to be a follower of Jesus.* Do you see the stark contrast in Paul's life? Paul was essentially a religious terrorist before he met Jesus. After he fell in love with Jesus, everything changed and all he wanted to do was preach the gospel and help build up leaders. Likewise, when our relationships change, we spring into action. You see, our love forms our identity.

Paul's New Identity (Romans 1:1)

Paul, a bond-servant of Christ Jesus, called as an apostle, set apart for the gospel of God.

Paul is writing this letter to the church in Rome, but in the introduction of this letter he says some very significant things about himself based on his personal transformation. He says he is a servant, an apostle, and one who is set apart. He begins by saying he is a "servant of Christ Jesus." He identifies his name and then explains his identity as he understood it. The Greek word Paul uses for "servant," *doulos*, is also translated "slave" or "bond-servant." It refers to a person who is obligated to serve a master. In Paul's time, it usually involved paying off a financial obligation. People were indebted to other rich individuals, and a *doulos* was required to pay them back through service to their master. Paul saw himself indebted to Jesus as a servant.

Paul also goes on to say that he is called to be an "apostle." The simplest definition of an apostle is "one who is sent." A king, for example, might send servants for specific services. Apostles in the New Testament were sent by King Jesus, in His authority, for His purposes. Apostles kept the gospel message clear, planted more churches, and wrote the letters that we now call the New Testament Scriptures. Paul was sent by Jesus to take the gospel to places where it hadn't been heard yet.

Paul viewed himself as a servant of Jesus, sent with Jesus's authority for a very specific purpose to deliver the message of the gospel. Paul articulates that purpose as being "set apart for the gospel of God." Paul viewed his life as one that is set apart for being completely about the gospel of God. This meant his entire life would be given over to this one purpose.

Paul sees himself with a new identity, as a servant of Christ. As he came to faith, Paul didn't just add Jesus into his life. He was set apart by God. His whole identity was reshaped for the purposes of Jesus. As Christians, just like Paul, we are all called servants of the King and servants of Christ. Just like Paul, we all find ourselves called by Jesus, on a mission. This mission is something that we have been uniquely gifted, wired, and anointed to do—something that we could not do and accomplish on our own, yet our wiring contributes to it. We all have a mission—something that excites us. As Christians, what should our service and mission look like? How are we to be set apart for the gospel? What would you do as one set apart by Jesus if time and money weren't a barrier?

Many years ago, I was sitting in a men's meeting, and the

pastor asked the group this question: "If you had all the time and the money in the world, what would get you out of bed in the morning?" My response was that I wanted to teach the Bible. But the pastor's question was a setup because the next question was, "Why aren't you doing it now?" After many years, I've found my mission. I've been blessed to teach people that the Bible has truth that is relevant for today. You have a purpose as one set apart by Jesus as well. It's my hope that throughout this study you will see more clearly how to partner with God for His purposes. But in order to be one who becomes a "bond-servant" and who is "set apart," we have to understand it within the context of the gospel—the good news that God came to rescue us from sin and death and put us on a mission.

God's Purpose and Plan (Romans 1:2)

Which He promised beforehand through His prophets in the holy Scriptures.

Did you know that God's gospel has always been His plan to engage our lives from the beginning? In Genesis 3, Adam and Eve failed miserably, but God proclaimed the gospel over them and over all of humanity by telling them there was a Christ to come. And as the promises of the Bible unfold, it becomes clear that God has for all of history been proclaiming Christ. In this place of history, we get to see it in our lives. Paul knows that he lives in an amazing time where the things of God that have been once promised are unfolded, told, seen, and realized. Paul is a partaker in the most amazing, highly anticipated promise of God. The church often misses this because we don't live in an era with firsthand witnesses of his death and resurrection. We live in an era of skepticism and mythology.

The ability to see God's accomplishment of a promised plan is important for our faith. When we find ourselves inside God's plan, we can understand that our lives have a designed purpose. When I came to faith, my life was messed up. I'm going to share that story in coming chapters. The big idea is that God came to me when I was in need. So when I read the Bible and the stories of Paul, I see God working in my life in a similar way. Paul's story gave me hope because he was a mess before he met Jesus. If God showed up in Paul's life, I have hope that he can show up in mine.

Similarly, when we're able to see Jesus's life foretold thousands of years before His coming, when we see this as history unfolding under the sovereign plan of God, then we can identify ourselves in the story and find our place and purpose with faith to understand that God is with us. If we see what God has accomplished in time past, through broken people like us, we can have faith to believe we're a part of God's plan in our own time. If God has used broken people in the past, then He can do the same with us. In fact, since there's no such thing as unbroken people, we are in good company.

Consider Paul. He was an individual who might have accomplished the most good for the first-century church among all the early church leaders. Yet he was also the worst of all, since he persecuted and killed Christians. He thought that he was pleasing God. If such a person can make such a splash on the first-century landscape, then how much more can God use us? How much more if we understand our own place in this unfolding plan?

Jesus the Christ, Son of God, Son of David, and Lord of All (Romans 1:3-6)

Concerning his Son, who was descended from David according to the flesh and was declared to be the Son of God in power according to the Spirit of holiness by his resurrection from the dead, Jesus Christ our Lord, through whom we have received grace and apostleship to bring about the obedience of faith for the sake of his name among all the nations, including you who are called to belong to Jesus Christ.

Who is Jesus according to these four verses? In the verses that came before, Paul outlined his own identity, and he outlines Jesus's identity as well. Jesus is "the Christ" as fulfillment of prophecy, He is human as the "Son of David," He is divine as the "Son of God," and He is resurrected as proof that he has authority over all as Lord.

Jesus Is Christ

Paul is a servant of "Christ Jesus." "Christ" is the Greek form of the Hebrew word *Messiah*, meaning the promised one of God. God had always had a promise that He was unveiling, unfolding, and accomplishing. Jesus is the fulfillment of all the promises of God. He is the Christ, the promised one, the Messiah, the one that would accomplish the unfolding promise of God revealed to us in Him. When we look at Scripture and we see God unfolding events, whether through people, types, symbols, or miracles, it fuels us to continue to look on at what God is going to do. But all of God's saving promises came bodily in Christ Jesus.

Jesus Is Human

Jesus is "descended from David according to the flesh." This is a fulfillment of a kingly, human lineage. Jesus became the King of all kings and the eternal Lord of all lords, but He also came in the flesh as promised in the Scriptures. Have you ever wondered why some Bible passages include long family trees? This is why. We can trace Jesus's family lineage and have confidence that He is the king we've been looking for.

Jesus Is Divine

Jesus is the "Son of God." Jesus is not only the chosen Anointed One and the Messiah, He is a human king, and He is simultaneously divine. Jesus made this claim of Himself many times in the gospels. For example, in John 8:58, Jesus was speaking to the Pharisees, saying, *"Before Abraham was, I Am."* The "I Am" title is in direct reference to a divine title God gave Himself when He spoke to Moses at the burning bush in Exodus 3:14.

Jesus Is Alive and Risen

Last, in His resurrection, Jesus gives us proof that He is who He says He is through His resurrection. People can make all kinds of claims about their resume, but Jesus is the only one who has raised Himself from the dead. When someone raises Himself from the dead, that's a good indication that He's someone worth listening to.

When you put these things together, that He is Messiah, human, divine, and resurrected, you have a man who is not 50 percent human and 50 percent divine, but 100 percent human and 100 percent divine. To our logic, the math doesn't add up, yet it's still true. And as the one who has risen from the dead, we have good reason to put our belief in Him.

God's Grace Gives Us a New Identity

What we see here is that Jesus does much more than will our salvation. He also sends us, like Paul, as bond-servants and messengers of the gospel. To be a Christian, it's imperative that we receive the good news message of the gospel. But put another way, when we ask the question, "Is loving Jesus enough?" again, we can never separate loving Jesus (and accepting the message of the gospel) from our own transformation (v. 5). To paraphrase verse 5, we receive grace and apostleship which in turn brings about obedience in us. Not just for our own sakes, but for the sake of proclaiming His name to others. In one sense, loving Jesus is enough, but it doesn't stop there. Our new identity in Jesus puts us into service to Him for the sake of the gospel. Paul tells us that we inherit our salvation, our grace, and our mission from God, through faith. As inheritors of grace, we experience salvation and are given an "apostolic" mission to go and tell the world about Jesus. We're not just given something to make us happy or bring us joy. Though Jesus freely gives us salvation, it changes who we are and it calls us to respond, and this creates an outcome of our faith. The outcome of receiving grace is that we get a new identity in Jesus. In turn, that identity gives us an outward focus. That outward focus is our mission. And every believer in Jesus is called to obedience to Him. That obedience leads to our transformation. This is for all who belong to Jesus.

When you fall in love with someone, it changes you. It's transforming. When I said, "I do," to my wife Lisa, when I said I wanted to be her husband for a lifetime, I was not misled to think that things wouldn't change. I went from being a single guy to being a married guy. That was an identity change. I fell in love with my wife, and it caused me to do new things, to care about things I had never cared about, to own things like dust ruffles, duvets, and stuff I had never even heard of. I didn't even know these words or the color mauve. Love caused me to give my life for something—for her—because love changes us. It changes our identity, our mission, and our purpose. Likewise, if you were to ask Paul if loving Jesus is enough of a response, he would undoubtedly say that unless our love has created a new identity, caused change, and given us purpose for the kingdom, then our love for Jesus has not gone far enough yet.

I find the most transformation in my life when I'm most in love with Jesus. Likewise, no one has to tell me that loving my wife means not treating her poorly, not speaking to her rudely, and being faithful to her. Love produces action. And when it comes to our faith, when we belong to Jesus and His mission, the outcome is faithful obedience to Him.

God's Grace Gives Us a Mission (Romans 1:7–8)

> *To all those in Rome who are loved by God and called to be saints: Grace to you and peace from God our Father and the Lord Jesus Christ. First, I thank my God through Jesus Christ for all of you, because your faith is proclaimed in all the world.*

I love that Paul doesn't skimp on telling the Roman church how much God loves them. He affirms that their faith is true, he thanks God for them, and even more, he calls them saints. This is not a reference to venerated saints the way that Roman

Catholics understand it. *Saint* is another word derived from the same word for "holy," which means "set apart." You and I, along with the entire Church, are saints loved by God, set apart by Him for His mission. We have been called for a purpose, for a mission, fueled by grace.

Notice that in Paul's letters *grace* always precedes *peace*. You will never find peace in this life apart from the grace of Christ. You must find yourself in Christ first. Then, as Paul will go on to say, you can have peace that surpasses understanding (Philippians 4:7). You can have peace inside your heart even when everything in your world says you should have no peace in this life. When everything is upside down, you can know that God's grace gives us peace. And we're going to need this peace for the mission we're called to.

Love Changes Everything

Before the letter to the Romans was put into the Bible, the members of the Roman church probably couldn't rub two Bible verses together to save their lives. But they were passionate about Jesus, they grew into a church, and their faith was made famous. They had never heard Jesus teach, and they didn't have a trained leader. Yet their church continued to grow, so much so that all over the world, the people were hearing about their faith. This means their faith was pointed out toward the world in missions. What does this mean for us? To bring this all full circle, it means what we love informs what we do.

Loving Jesus is absolutely what it means to be a Christian. It also has natural implications, because loving another always transforms who we are. In this letter to the Romans, Paul's love was redirected toward Jesus, and he became a missionary. In my case, when I committed to my wife Lisa in marriage, it meant that my love was demonstrated in loving service to her. You can't love someone else and not be changed. Parents remember these moments. When you find out you're pregnant, you hear the baby's heartbeat; and when the baby is born, parents are forever changed by love for their child.

Jesus says it like this in the Gospel of John: *"If you love me, you will keep my commandments."* For way too long this passage has been understood incorrectly. It doesn't say, "If you love me, *then* I want you to keep my commandments." It says to love Jesus first and then obedience to Him will follow. When we love Jesus, things change. When we love someone, our hearts are inclined toward action. Our purpose and our mission in life get focused. Is loving Jesus enough? Yes, absolutely. But if you look at your confession of love and it's not transforming you, then I would ask more questions about what your love for Jesus means.

What Would You Do in Life If Money Weren't an Issue?

Earlier in this chapter I'd mentioned a conversation that focused my Christian life. A pastor once asked me, "If you had all the time and the money in the world, what would get you out of bed in the morning?" My answer was that I wanted to teach the Bible. By God's grace, I've been given a great opportunity to see that desire become a reality. Now, let me pose that question to you: what do *you* love? If time, money and resources weren't a barrier for you, what would *you* do? You, me, the Apostle Paul—we are all set apart and uniquely gifted for the sake of the gospel. We've identified that our loves create our identities. With that in mind, how are you now set apart for the gospel in your own life? Think about how marriage changes our identities. Now, how is God using you and how you're uniquely gifted to bring the good news to others? However you answer those questions, let me encourage you: you will never regret being used by Jesus in this life.

ARE ALL SINS EQUAL?

Romans 1:18–2:11

Are all sins equal, or does God treat one sin as greater than another? Are some people more guilty than others in God's eyes?

If you spend any amount of time at Generations Church, you'll notice this is a diverse group of people who come from many walks of life. We have business owners and bikers, great-grandparents and college students, soccer moms and recovering addicts. We have people of many ethnicities, socio-economic positions, liberals and conservatives, people in suits and others in shorts. You name it, we have it. On any given Sunday you might find very different cultures colliding, including police officers sitting next to ex-convicts, and right wing conservatives sitting next to someone from the LGBT community. We have people attend who are committed in same sex marriages and one who was born a man but dresses as a woman.

When we consider the question, "Are all sins equal?" at Generations Church, it's a relevant question to ask because there can be so many people from different walks of life attending at any time. We live in a culture today that has highly varied ideologies on this particular topic, and the church at large hasn't done a good job of responding to this. For example, you might walk into a church where a rainbow flag is on display in the sanctuary as a way to show that they affirm same sex union. Other churches are strong and vocal in their convictions on this subject, and stand for traditional, one-man-one-woman marriage. These folks may be combative toward those on the "progressive" side of the issue who might fly a rainbow flag. For those who would otherwise be curious about the Bible and about Christianity, how are they to make sense of the issues that seem to be so divisive among Christian believers?

If you're straight, imagine you're gay and you go to church. How would you be exposed to the gospel? How would these dividing issues make you feel? I have gay relatives, and I wonder what their church-going experience would be. Can we engage these issues? I believe so.

As a pastor, I feel frustrated about how the church engages these hot button topics. Instead, the church often gives frustrating, shallow answers to the tough questions of life. One church answers the issue of same-sex attraction by accepting it and redefining the parts of Scripture that speak against it, while it seems that another church takes the biblical statements more literally, yet seems to hold that this particular "sin" is different, as if God hates this more than other sins. Despite all these dividing lines, I do think the Bible offers satisfying answers to people asking these tough questions. As followers of Jesus, there must be a faithful way to live amid all of the controversy.

Romans chapter 1 contains what can be a very controversial

passage today, but I suggest that the controversy is often brought on by how we approach Scripture itself. Examining the passage in its context rather than through the lens of today's biases makes all the difference in the world. As we begin to examine the latter part of Romans chapter 1, here are 3 questions to consider: 1.) Are all sins equal? 2.) Does God treat one sin as greater than another? 3.) Are some people guiltier than others in God's eyes?

Laying the Gospel Groundwork

The truth is, different churches treat sins in different ways. But before we dive deeper into answering these questions, I want to lay some groundwork. The gospel is ultimately the answer to all of these hard questions. In order to move the conversation forward, we need a strong definition of what "gospel" means. My simple definition of the gospel is what is traditionally referred to as Creation, Fall, Redemption, and Restoration.[1]

Creation

First, God created and designed the world and all mankind in love. For all of humanity there is a design, a way we are created to live. Simply put, we were designed to be worshipers of God. This means that all we do should bring honor and glory to our Creator.

---

1. In place of *restoration*, some historical church documents use the word *consummation*.

Fall

Second, we have all failed to live according to God's design as stated above. Human history shows that every human being, from Adam to the present, has fallen short of God's design. We have inherited guilt and contributed to the collective guilt of humanity, and we all know it. Few people think to themselves, "I've never done anything wrong." We've all done things wrong purposefully and by accident. Simply, we've all failed God's design for how to live in the world. We are both born under all of this sin, and we contribute to the collective sin of the world as well.

Redemption

Third, Jesus came and sacrificed his perfect life for our sinful lives. Jesus came and lived faithfully and fully the way that God designed human beings to live. Jesus sacrificed his perfect life. We exchange our brokenness for Christ's righteousness. As He hung between heaven and earth, between God and man, He became the mediator drawing us back to our Creator. In Christ our lives truly can have redemption.

Restoration

Fourth, God calls us back to living how we were created to live. In this, God begins to restore all things. Through no effort of our own, we are restored by Christ and empowered by the Spirit. Jesus not only forgives us, but in His resurrection He gives us new life.

The Creation, Fall, Redemption, and Restoration motif is where we need to see ourselves in the context of this highly controversial Romans passage. When we look through the lens of the gospel, through a redemptive historical narrative using these terms above, it allows us to see this passage in its intended context. Remember, all of us were born after The Fall, and none of us was born before humanity was infected with sin. We are all recipients of this death and are all in need of redemption and restoration.

Not Ashamed of the Gospel (Romans 1:16–17)

For I am not ashamed of the gospel, for it is the power of God for salvation to everyone who believes, to the Jew first and also to the Greek. For in it the righteousness of God is revealed from faith for faith, as it is written, "The righteous shall live by faith."

Paul begins with the same understanding: we were created to live differently than we do, and we are all born under the weight of the sin of millennia of human history. He also knows that the gospel is sufficient to remedy the problem. However, consider this before we go too far: knowing that God has designed us and knows best how we are to live means that, when we live differently from how God has designed, we are saying, "God, I know what's best for my life. You don't." We become the god of our life and push the God who created us away.

When Paul says, "I am not ashamed of the gospel," he is willing to proclaim that what God has said is true when God said it, is true in Paul's day, and by implication is also true in our day. Paul is proclaiming this in such a way to challenge us today. Is God still true in our time and place? Is Romans still applicable and relevant for us? Is the Bible something that can still be relied upon today? Paul would absolutely say yes.

I come from a rough background. In the past, I've lived very differently from how I do now. I wasn't a Christian growing up; I came to follow Jesus as an adult. Even as a Christian I haven't always followed what I know God calls me to do. But I can tell you that every time I follow God's way, even when I don't understand, God has proved Himself to be right. Believing that God is right doesn't mean that living the Christian life is easy; in fact, sometimes following God can make life more difficult when we refuse to take shortcuts. Can we be bold enough to join Paul in saying, "I am not ashamed of the gospel," no matter where it takes us?

To Both Jew and Greek

What was the significant difference between Jews and Greeks at that time? The Jews were a monotheistic community who believed in the God of the Bible, whereas the Romans lived very differently and were considered outsiders by the Jewish community. The Romans were heavily influenced by the polytheistic Greek culture. Paul's message of the gospel brought these different groups of people together because his message isn't about who you are or what you do, but about what God does for us. It is for anyone desiring to pursue God by faith. The gospel is for anyone from any background or lifestyle, raised in the church or not. It was "first for the Jew" because it was calling Jewish people to follow Jesus as a fulfillment of the Scriptures.

That the power of the gospel was also for the "Greek" means it is also for those outside the Jewish faith. Greek culture was polytheistic and had a very different understanding of sex, gender, and sexuality than the Jewish culture did. The gospel is for everyone. This is why we have all types of people attending Generations Church each Sunday. Some lean ideologically left; some lean right. We have young and old, and many who believe different things about specific political or ideological issues. In verse 17, Paul says, "This is the power of the gospel" for anyone who would believe, no matter your religious background or ideological persuasion. The gospel is for everyone.

"Righteousness and Faith"

Righteousness and faith are terms frequently used in the Bible, but not often used the same way in society today. Paul says the gospel shows us the righteousness of God. But what does "righteousness" mean? "Righteousness" is the quality of being morally right or justified. We have to ask the question, through the lens of the gospel, how do we find God to be morally right or justified? Before we answer that question, let's consider what we've covered so far.

We began this chapter by defining the gospel in four terms: Creation, Fall, Redemption, Restoration. Creation proclaims that there is a God who designed us and that we flourish when we live as He created us to live. The opposite is also true: God says that if we live opposed to our design, it will only cause trouble, pain, and separation from our Creator. Yet admittedly we've all lived our own way.

We all know there are laws that govern how we live. It is for the wellbeing of all of us that those laws exist. We also know that if we break those laws there needs to be a penalty. And when we break those laws it affects people. It affects our neighbors and ourselves. As I said above, I didn't always live the Christian life. In fact, I grew up on the wrong side of the law. I was in a lot of trouble in the 80s and 90s, and there came a time when a judge was about to sentence me. I'd been wrong and lived contrary to God's will. The judge would have done the "righteous" thing to sentence me for the crimes I'd committed. I'll tell more about my story later in this book as it applies. But all this to say, we can see God's righteousness when we know we're on the wrong side of God's law. So in light of this righteousness, what is morally right or justifiable?

Which of the two is morally right or justifiable? Paul says that in the gospel God shows His righteousness. But it's not in the way we expect. It's here that we get to see this redemptive side of God's righteousness. Just like a judge who is lenient in sentencing someone deserving punishment, God can also show His character in either penalty or lenience.

Let's summarize a bit of what it means to live the way God designed us to live. I call this living lives of worship. This means lives of holiness that are set apart for God as we spoke about in the last chapter. It does not mean lives of perfection, but lives given over to God. A life given over to God means all aspects of life belong to Him. That means our speech, our sexuality, and our worship. If God created us, then God gets to tell us how we are created to live.

The Great Exchange

In 2 Corinthians 5:19–21, Paul addresses righteousness this way:

> *That is, in Christ God was reconciling the world to himself, not counting their trespasses against them, and entrusting to us the message of reconciliation. Therefore, we are*

ambassadors for Christ, God making his appeal through us. We implore you on behalf of Christ, be reconciled to God. For our sake he made him to be sin who knew no sin, so that in him we might become the righteousness of God.

How does this Scripture show God as righteous? It's here where Jesus trades His perfect life for ours. It's because Jesus lived fully how God has called us to live. Where we failed, Jesus was victorious. Jesus willingly traded His perfect life for broken and sinful lives like yours and mine.

But we sinners still have a just penalty coming our way. How is it just or righteous of God to let us "off the hook"? Think about it this way: if a young man stole from a store and was caught, the judge would be justified to give him his due punishment. But what if the young man's dad stepped in and said he wanted to stand in the gap for his son? Then imagine the judge and the father work together to make things right again. Wouldn't the judge be just and righteous in finding a way to work with the dad and the young man? Of course! We all want to see people step up, own mistakes, grow, and get second chances. God is the judge, and He does mete out punishment, but Jesus stands up and willingly takes that punishment in our place. This exchange is the "righteousness of God." God is righteous because the penalty for sin has been paid, and God is merciful because Jesus takes the penalty on our behalf.

On the cross, more than a death took place. There is more than the scourging that anticipates a crucifixion. There is more than the nails driven through hands and feet as the onlookers mocked Jesus. What happened there on the cross was God pouring out his wrath against *all our sin* on Jesus. Jesus cried out, *"My God, my God, why have you forsaken me?"* (Mark 15:34). Jesus asks God, "Why have you turned your back on me?" Jesus had always been face to face with God, and there at the cross He felt God's abandonment. That's because Jesus had to receive the wrath of God so that we wouldn't have to. A benevolent, gracious, and merciful God gives us the opportunity to either be covered by Christ having the wrath of God satisfied in Christ, or stand on our own and receive the wrath of God personally. You see, there is justice, there is moral fairness, and there is righteousness. God says to you and me, "You are guilty, and you deserve my wrath, but I have provided a way out."

We were created by God to give worship and obedience to God. This is what human beings were designed to do. Anything other than living by that demand is idolatry. Idolatry is making ourselves god in place of the real God. It is putting ourselves in a place that only God our Creator deserves to be. Idolatry is a denial of God. So, would God be righteous to punish us? Absolutely. However, God our gracious Father steps in and makes things right. God is righteous in finding both a way to take our penalty and in reconciling us to Himself. That is what takes place in the gospel.

Paul says that it's in the gospel that we see the righteousness of God, that we see the goodness, the quality of being morally right or justified. We see the penalty of sin paid for, but also grace in not condemning all of humanity for all their sins without some way to find redemption. Peter says it this way: *"For Christ also suffered once for sins, the righteous for the unrighteous that he might bring us to God being put to death in the flesh but made alive in the spirit"* (1 Peter 3:18).

The Wrath of God (Romans 1:18)

For the wrath of God is revealed from heaven against all ungodliness and unrighteousness of men, who by their unrighteousness suppress the truth.

Here's the problem: in our modern-day church culture, the gospel often presents a very watered down version of God. He is portrayed as this loving and benevolent God. However, God is also holy and just. When we deserve a penalty, it would be unholy, unjust, and even unrighteous for us not to receive a penalty. In our modern mindset, we don't like to talk about deserving the wrath of God. But we're OK if we're talking about someone like a terrorist or Hitler. For most of us, we don't like to believe that we deserve the wrath of God. But according to this verse, Paul is stating that all of us deserve wrath because none of us is righteous (Romans 3:10). We love when the Bible says that God loved us so much that He gave us Jesus (John 3:16). However, we don't always like the part that follows two verses later, that says that whoever doesn't believe in Jesus "is condemned" (John 3:18).

We love to talk about the positive attributes of God—His salvation, His grace, His mercy, and how we get blessing and healing from Him. We love this because we are the recipient and only want good things to happen to us. Who wants the wrath of God poured out on them? Not me! However, consider that without something "bad," salvation is meaningless. The term salvation implies that we are saved *from* something. What are we actually to be saved from? Take the story of Noah's Ark as an example.

We love the story of Noah's ark because there's a positive

outcome in which God does a loving and kind thing by saving humanity and protecting nature. To be fair though, Noah's story wouldn't make much sense without a flood. Without a flood, Noah is just a guy on dry land with a big boat that smells like animal poop.

In the same way, there's no salvation if there is no wrath of God. Wouldn't the cross be a waste of time if there was no wrath of God? We all want to celebrate what we are saved *to*, and we all want to hear that God loves us, justifies us, saves us freely by grace and mercy because we're undeserving. That's all true, but he must be saving us *from* something. God is saving us from His wrath.

Paul says later in Romans 5:8–9, *"But God shows his love for us in that while we were still sinners, Christ died for us. Since, therefore, we have now been justified by his blood, much more shall we be saved by him from the wrath of God."* In other words, without the wrath of God, without something horribly bad, without the penalty, salvation is without power and meaning. There's nothing "to be saved from." Paul underscores this by saying, *"For if while we were enemies we were reconciled to God by the death of his Son, much more, now that we are reconciled, shall we be saved by his life"* (Romans 5:10). Most people today, even Christians, don't believe they start out as enemies of God, born under the wrath of God and separated from Him. Today most believe that we start out neutral, and somehow God grades on a curve. We might hear someone say something like, "I know I'm not Mother Teresa, but I'm also not Hitler." Most of us believe we're "good people." Sadly, that is not a biblical perspective.

The gospel says that even though God created, loved, and designed us, we all live in disobedience to His design. Later in chapter 3, Paul writes, *"For all have sinned and fall short of the glory of God"* (Romans 3:23). All of us are due the wrath of God. We misunderstand who we are and, consequently, what our due punishment should be. It isn't until you get a handle on the wrath of God that you really begin to appreciate the salvation of God. Jesus says, *"Those who have been forgiven much love much"* (Luke 7:47).

Not only do modern Christians stray away from the reality that we all deserve God's wrath, they also fail to see the incredible gospel promise given to us. In spite of all this, God loves you, and He sent Jesus to save you. Understanding the heaviness of Noah's story helps us understand God's great love in rescuing Noah.

Do All Sins Deserve Wrath?

What sins is Paul saying deserve of the wrath of God? Is it that only some sins are due wrath and not others? Paul says, "All unrighteousness and ungodliness." Not just *some* sin, but *all* sin deserves wrath. God isn't pleased with some sins, irritated with others, and wrathful against the worst ones. We see God's wrath against all sin. Either God's wrath is taken out on our Savior Jesus Christ or on us. All of us are on a level playing field when it comes to being sinful and due God's wrath.

To receive salvation means being spared God's wrath through Jesus taking it on Himself. Paul says God's wrath is being poured out on all unrighteousness and ungodliness. Then Paul singles out one specific issue of unrighteousness—namely, the suppression of truth, which is his theme for several verses. We all have lists of sins we think are worse than others. But whatever list we come up with, it's not likely that we include "suppressing the truth."

Suppressing the Truth (Romans 1:19–20)

Because that which is known about God is evident within them; for God made it evident to them. For since the creation of the world His invisible attributes, His eternal power and divine nature, have been clearly seen, being understood through what has been made, so that they are without excuse.

If you have two eyes, Paul says you're without excuse for failing to see God revealed in our world. As an example, I can't walk outside into my driveway and see a vehicle without realizing someone created it. I don't have to be an engineer in computer science to understand that someone made my computer. Someone made the watch that I wear, and the car that I drive, so we are prone to understanding that everything is "made" and has a design. It also makes sense that if I use something in an unintended way, I am likely to destroy it. I have both a Harley-Davidson motorcycle, and a Jeep. One is made to tow things, and the other is not. If I were to try to tow my Jeep with my Harley, I would have some serious problems. However, my Jeep is made with the ability and design to tow. I can tow the Harley with the Jeep, but not the other way around. Clearly God's design for our lives matters.

I fully believe that we can't honestly look around and say to ourselves that this planet is just an amazing accident. That doesn't mean that we can't have real dialogue about science and creation, but we must eventually come to the conclusion that something or someone had to get our world started. Even if you believe that somehow a random, scientific anomaly jump-started the first one-celled amoeba, then millions of years later—Bang!—you have human beings, you've got to at least ask yourself where the bang came from and what caused it all to start. This isn't a science debate, and I don't want to discredit people's questions. The point is, we're all without excuse, and we are designed to live a certain way because of God's design.

Darkened Minds (Romans 1:21)

For although they knew God they did not honor him as God or give thanks to him, but they became futile in their thinking and their foolish hearts were darkened.

When we ignore that there is a Creator God, we also ignore the Creator's design (given to us by the designer), and we begin to think we're greater than God. In the process, our thinking becomes futile and our hearts are darkened. Someone sent me a ten-minute YouTube clip that I watched recently. The speaker was saying that Scripture may have been true at one time, but we've since moved on to have clearer understanding, as if we've advanced right past God. Today we deem ourselves smarter, more evolved, or culturally wiser than God, which is proof that our minds have become futile and darkened. If the Scriptures were true at one time, they're just as true and relevant for today. For all our so-called evolution and progress for the better, why is the world still so broken? Paul asserts that if we live against the design of God, and we embrace it as normal or right, then it shows us that our hearts have been hardened and our thinking is flawed. This is where Paul pivots to develop his main point.

All Sin Is Rooted in Idolatry (Romans 1:22-23)

Claiming to be wise they became fools and exchanged the glory of the immortal God for images resembling mortal man and birds and animals and creeping things.

The Roman people were quite religious, but they were in no way monotheistic. They believed in many gods and were very superstitious. There were statues of idols all over public spaces. When we think of idolatry, this kind of scene makes sense. But though our Western cultural context is different, the concept of idolatry still applies today.

Biblically defined, idolatry is loving anything more than God. Anytime we take God off the throne metaphorically by placing anything else there, we are making an idol of that thing. They can be good things in our lives like our spouse, kids, vocation, education, income, status, or whatever. Or it could be an actual wood or gold image. Paul's point is that all sin is rooted in idolatry because it is wrongly placed worship.

Every time I fall short of what God has called me to, I am choosing something over God, and that something becomes an idol. Letting my job control my life is just as bad as bowing down to a golden calf. If I allow the sin of lust, jealousy, selfishness, love of money, or anything else to be what guides me, I might as well be worshiping a statue of Buddha or Zeus.

So, as Paul states, *"God gave them up to the lust of their hearts."* This is a controversial cultural topic right now, but Paul is writing to Christians who are part of a church in Rome. The setting of the first century is one of huge sexual diversity, much like our own, and the church in Rome was no different from the world around it. In the church that Paul is writing to they are living as sexually diverse as the Roman world around them, and their cultural landscape looks much the same as ours.

Sex and Worship (Romans 1:24-25)

Therefore God gave them up to the lust of their hearts, to impurity, to the dishonor in their bodies among themselves because they exchanged the truth about God for a lie and worshipped and served the creature rather than the creator who is blessed forever. Amen.

Paul writes to the men and women in Rome particularly and specifically when he writes this. Paul explains that they have traded in the Creator for the creation and have exchanged the glory of the immortal God for something that's far less satisfying and worthy. When our worship gets skewed, good God-created things like sex become our God. We do this today too. When we allow anything in our lives to define us, we are allowing something created instead of our Creator to define who we really are and who He has intended us to be.

The Problem with Isolating "Pet Sins" (Romans 1:26-27)

For this reason God gave them up to dishonorable passions. For their women exchanged natural relations for those that are contrary to nature; and the men likewise gave up natural relations with women and were consumed with passion for one another, men committing shameless acts with men and receiving in themselves the due penalty for their error.

Paul is addressing a specific sin in the Roman culture to identify their idolatry. If Paul were to write to the church today, he could use a similar example. However, Paul could just as easily address the rampant use of pornography in the church today as well. Paul says God designed humanity to live a certain way, and "they"—people within the Roman church—exchanged that for relationships with those of the same gender. God identifies both men and women and calls this shameful.

This definitely applies to the church today and our own context. We have divisions in the church because we understand these issues differently. You have both liberal and conservative readings of this passage. I serve as the pastor of a fairly conservative theological church, though neither the church nor I look like the typical conservative church. As a critique of my own "theological tribe," the problem with conservative churches like ours is the tendency to isolate one sin and treat it as the worst thing ever. Often those of us who trend theologically conservative can lack grace and love. We cherry pick passages like this one to make a case, and in the process we get it all wrong.

On the other side of this, those who tend to be more theologically liberal ignore or redefine whole passages of Scripture in order to make Christianity more palatable. All they've really done is water down the gospel. Paul is holding up the biblical view of a one-man-one-woman marriage for a lifetime. But Paul isn't singling this out as if this issue is worse than others. He's just calling out this one issue of how the Roman church was trading in true, God-honoring worship for idolatry.

But again, Paul is writing to a specific church, struggling with specific sin—particularly the sin of suppressing the truth. Consider that today people on both sides of the biblical sexuality debate tend toward "suppressing the truth." The conservative church suppresses the truth about God loving, saving, rescuing, redeeming, and transforming people who have different sexuality practices from their own. They're too hung up on one kind of sin. The liberal church misses the call to holiness, redemption, and restoration. They suppress the truth of the life transformation that takes place in Christ. Both miss pieces of the gospel.

Paul wrote this before science understood that people could be born with a proclivity toward particular lifestyles or struggles, like homosexuality or addiction as two examples. But that doesn't change this passage. If we understand that we are all born under the fall, meaning we are all born broken, then people are absolutely born with inherent tendencies that are antithetical to living a God-honoring life. Of course people are born broken and sinful.

If we are prone toward a particular proclivity to sin, this doesn't change our design given to us by God (we'll address these issues in more detail in chapters 3 and 5). Our design, which dictates how we best live and flourish, predates sin entering into human history. It predates our brokenness. When we allow any part of us to exist in contrast to God's design, we will worship that part of us that wants to be apart from God. Sexuality is a powerful example of this because it can become someone's entire identity, even within the church.

Paul says not to exchange worship of the eternal God for worship in the moment. For decades, Christianity has singled this passage out for being one that clearly teaches against homosexuality. Though that is factually true, it completely misses the point. This is a passage about trading in worship of God for worship of something created, which could be a plethora of things in any era.

Given Over to a Clouded (Debased) Mind (Romans 1:28–31)

And since they did not see fit to acknowledge God, God gave them up to a debased mind to do what ought not to be done. They were filled with all manner of unrighteousness, evil, covetousness, malice. They are full of envy, murder, strife, deceit, maliciousness. They are gossips, slanderers, haters of God, insolent, haughty, boastful, inventors of evil, disobedient to parents, foolish, faithless, heartless, ruthless.

The example Paul uses about sexual sin is relevant to the Roman church because it's profoundly impacted by this one thing. But he doesn't stop there. The same people who suppress the truth are full of envy, murder, strife and maliciousness. They are gossipers and slanderers, haters of God, insolent, haughty, boastful, inventors of evil, disobedient to parents. They are foolish, faithless, heartless, and ruthless.

"They" are those who suppress the truth, those who trade in worship of God for worship of created things. Remember to whom Paul is writing: the church of believers and followers of Jesus. If he were addressing our church today, he would list something more profoundly impactful than this. He would likely write about sexual sin because that's an issue in our culture as well. He would probably identify premarital sex, extramarital sex, and pornography, alongside same-sex attraction. Women caught up in chat rooms and romantic conversation with those who are not their husbands would not be let off the hook either. Men looking at airbrushed images of other women in pornography would most likely be taken aim at too. He would aim at our church, not the church in Rome, and he would hit us as hard as he hit them. Because we too trade in worship of the Creator for worship of all kinds of created things.

Our Sins = Death (Romans 1:32)

Though they know God's righteous decrees that those who practice such things deserve to die, they not only do them but give approval to those who practice them.

The "they" are all the people doing those things listed. He likens those who are gossips and slanderers to those who are sexually sinful. And he says they are all deserving of death! This isn't a death penalty like we think of it. This is an eternal death.

You might wonder why someone who gossips is liable for an eternal death penalty, but consider that this is neither about sexual sin nor sins of speech. This is about trading in worship of God for worship of created things. This is about the reality that trading the things of this world, whether in word or deed, means trading in God Himself for something or someone else. This is not only false worship, but it is outright denial of God. Paul goes so far as to say that we know better and we suppress the truth.

Judge Yourself First (Romans 2:1–3)

Therefore you have no excuse, O man, every one of you who judges. For in passing judgment on another you condemn yourself, because you, the judge, practice the very same things. We know that the judgment of God rightly falls on those who practice such things. Do you suppose oh man you who judge those who practice such things and yet do them yourself that you will escape the judgment of God?

Contrary to how some believe, this passage doesn't say we can't judge right or wrong. In fact, throughout Scripture we are commanded to judge and discern. What Paul is really saying is to judge yourself first and find where you're guilty of these things. If I am guilty of any sexual sin, I am to judge myself first, not the outside world. That doesn't mean that I can't look at the outside world and say that the world's not moving in a direction toward God. It just causes me to take an honest assessment of myself, and not spend my days only pointing out the flaws of others.

If I'm to look at the outside world and dislike how people use their speech hatefully, I should be assessing my own speech first. Am I a gossip or slanderer? Am I untruthful? If I don't judge myself first, I shouldn't go around judging others. But, by the same understanding, I don't have to be perfect to critique the world and those around me. It's how I approach this that makes all the difference. It is my own understanding of my sinfulness and brokenness that allows me to either rightly (or wrongly) discern the world around me. I am sinful and broken. I only stand before God with a secure foundation because I stand in Christ. Do I measure myself rightly or only the outside world around me? We're called to measure ourselves first in God's sight.

The number-one thing church outsiders say about Christians is that they are hypocrites. Why? Because we love to point out the things others are doing wrong, while ignoring the wrongs we do! We love to judge the speech of others, but not our own. We love to judge the sin of others, but not our own. This is not an excuse for us to overlook sin. We are not absolved of responsibility. This is a call for us to seek restoration, not only in our own lives but in our community. You have to start with your own heart first.

God's Kindness Leads Us to Repentance (Romans 2:4)

Do you presume on the riches of his kindness and forbearance and patience knowing that God's kindness is meant to lead you to repentance? Do you not know that it's the kindness of God that leads a man toward repentance?

This is one of my favorite gospel verses for today's culture. Often in sermons I've griped and vented about Christians who ask the common evangelism phrase to unbelievers, "If you died tonight, can you be sure you'd go to heaven?" Similarly there's a traveling group that goes around with bright yellow signs bearing derogatory, hateful messages. We've all seen them. These signs always list out specific sins, and their message is judgmental. What we don't see in either approach is the kindness of God. What Paul reminds me of right here is that I was led to Jesus by the love of God, not by the fear of hell. God called us in His kindness to go out and love our neighbor, love the lost, and love our community so that they never see the wrath of God. Do you not know that God's "kindness and forbearance and patience" are what ought to lead *you* to repentance?

What Does This Mean for Us Today? (Romans 2:11)

For God shows no partiality.

We've considered the question, "Is loving God enough?" It's true that there's nothing we can add to salvation, but it is also true that our salvation should transform us. We ought to be experiencing change in our lives. It doesn't matter if you come to faith when you're young or old. When you meet Jesus, it doesn't matter if you are gay or straight. It doesn't matter where your starting point in life is. Everyone needs change equally. We're all equally far away from God. Transformation is a piece of the puzzle. Jesus through the power of the gospel seeks to transform every one of us in the ways that are relevant to us, in the ways that we are far from God. God shows no partiality over sin, but clearly He judges the church for the sins of suppressing the truth that He calls them to.

When I meet with someone who struggles with their sexuality, I can relate because of my own issues of sin, even if they're very different from my own. We're all messed up, and we all need Jesus. It's in Christ that I find freedom and forgiveness. It's in Christ that I've been changed, and you can be too. Never am I better than anybody else. God calls us to judge ourselves in this area first before we choose to judge the world around us. That doesn't absolve us from calling people to truth. We're called to change ourselves and live in transparency with others. Everything goes away when we begin to obey God. Then we can say with surety and with clarity that there is a way to live. Not only do we have direction and design, but we have Jesus to look to.

How do we learn to lead people to Jesus rather than push them away by focusing on their brand of sin? How do we focus on truth and the reality that none of us live perfect lives? We point toward Christ in hope. He created us and loves us. He satisfied everything God needed for Him to begin to transform our lives and make them look more like Christ's.

DOES GOD WANT ONLY GOOD PEOPLE?

Romans 3:1–26

None of us are good, and all of us are in need of a Savior. Though it's a tough pill to swallow, knowing the depth of our fallen nature helps us to understand our need for a Savior.

I came to faith in a two-man jail cell, just before being sent back to prison. I finally got out of prison just before my 30th birthday, and I felt as if I had wasted so many years. I wondered to myself if I had thrown away any opportunity to have a good career, a good marriage, or a good faith. I was only thirty years old at the time, but I felt as if my life had been wasted. Now, almost two decades later, much has happened. Now I have hope, and I look forward to each next year. But at 30, I felt like a wreck and didn't know what was next for my life.

Leading up to my prison time, I had been a drug addict for 15 years. Drugs led to crime, crime led to jail, jail led to affiliations that kept me in and out of jails and prisons. At one point, I was in prison more than I was out of prison. I was committing crimes that were violent enough to lock me up forever if I'd gotten caught.

At the time, I was sadly OK with where my life was—and that was a big problem. In my heart, I had resigned myself to believing that I was never going to change. One day, I was sitting in my jail cell and I prayed a simple prayer: "God, if you can fix this life, I'll never leave you." At the time, some of my court cases hadn't been settled yet and the outcome was unclear. When I said that prayer, I wasn't sure I was getting out. I wasn't praying that I would get out of jail, in fact I was somewhat resigned to not getting out. I was really praying because I was scared of who I had become. I didn't know if that meant I would be following God in or out of prison, or even if I was going to get out of prison. What I did know is that I was a broken person.

Maybe you don't have the kind of background I do, but we all have struggles with questions of faith. In that prison cell, I did a lot of thinking. One question that kept coming to mind was, does God only love good people? If you're not a "good person" what do we have to change in order for God to love us? Before we get to picking apart the idea of being a "good person," let's consider what Romans chapter 3 has to say on the subject. What's the definition of a "good person" and does anyone have an advantage in "being good" over anyone else? Maybe being a good person requires being raised up in the right kind of family. Maybe it's all about attending the right school or belonging to the right religion. What makes someone good? Let's see what Romans chapter 3 has to say about it.

Is There an Advantage to a Good Start in Life? (Romans 3:1-2)

Then what advantage has the Jew? Or what is the value of circumcision? Much in every way. To begin with, the Jews were entrusted with the oracles of God.

Most commentators believe the church in Rome began from a Jewish convert to Christianity at Pentecost (we will get there in a minute) who went home to Rome with their newfound faith. Imagine what kind of gospel message might have been so compelling to make someone transform his faith so radically that he traveled back home, and through him many people came to faith.

Now, fast-forward to the church in Rome. Because Christianity has its roots in Judaism, Jewish believers would travel to Rome to tell the Roman Christians how to live their faith out. One such group of people were the Judaizers, a group of people who believed that, in order to be a good Christian, you had to be a good Jew first. One of the main practices that Jews adhered to was circumcision of all male infants. Now, with those ideas in mind, reread verses 1-2. Is there any advantage to being born Jewish? Paul's answer might seem odd, but his answer is "yes," there is benefit to being a Jew. He says this because they were entrusted with "the oracles of God" or, put another way, God's promises.

Let's ask the question from the vantage point of our own culture. Is there a benefit to having Christian parents? Absolutely. Why? Because parents can teach their kids what they know about Jesus. But what if you didn't have Christian parents? Could you still become a follower of Jesus? Yes, of course! While it would be helpful to grow up Christian, it's not absolutely necessary.

Take me as an example: when I came to faith in Jesus, I had a head start in many ways. Though I was exposed to Christianity as a kid, it was a more constricted, rules-based Christianity. My parents loved me and prayed for me. Sometimes, when I went to church, I did learn some things. There were rules in my dad's house that we had to read the Bible everyday, and when I lived with him for a couple years, I did. Some of my Bible knowledge stuck with me.

When I got out of prison at 30 years old, I had a whole lifetime of doing things wrong. But there were some good things embedded in me from growing up with a Christian background. When Paul asks, "What value is it to be a Jew?" and we consider that question from our own cultural standpoint, there are many advantages to growing up in a religious context.

What If You Grew Up with a Flawed View of Christianity? (Romans 3:3–8)

What if some were unfaithful? Does their faithlessness nullify the faithfulness of God? By no means! Let God be true though every one were a liar, as it is written, "That you may be justified in your words, and prevail when you are judged." But if our unrighteousness serves to show the righteousness of God, what shall we say? That God is unrighteous to inflict wrath on us? (I speak in a human way.) By no means! For then how could God judge the world? But if through my lie God's truth abounds to his glory, why am I still being condemned as a sinner? And why not do evil that good may come?—as some people slanderously charge us with saying. Their condemnation is just.

Notice here that these verses are addressing the subject of God's wrath, and we've covered this issue in the previous chapter thoroughly. In this passage, Paul is speaking to specific issues between the Judaizers and the Christians in Rome. We don't need to pick all of that apart; instead, let's address the pieces of this chapter that relate to our chapter question: "Does God only want good people?"

The church I went to as a teenager was by no means perfect, and neither was my family. We had a lot of brokenness in our home. In addition, the era of the late 1970s and early 1980s was a tough one on the church in America as well. There were many Christian leaders who failed publicly, some of whom we will talk about in a later chapter. There was a very legalistic (rules-driven) version of Christianity prevailing. Even still, I learned good things about Jesus through my family. The church communicated the message of Jesus, though sometimes in a very flawed way. Let's use this as an example to understand these six verses and the next few as well.

First off, did an un-perfect church or family "nullify" my learning about the truth of Jesus? No. In fact I learned a lot about Jesus and the Bible, even though I didn't follow through with faith at the time. So, God was able to use what I learned even when some of the context I learned it in was imperfect.

This was the era of televangelists who had some very public problems as well. What Paul is noting here is that even though they were wrong for living in duplicitous ways, some people actually heard about Jesus through them! This doesn't excuse their behavior, but shows God's power through the brokenness.

Without getting too far into the weeds in this passage, I want to address a piece of this passage that relates to our question for this chapter. Paul's question deals with right and wrong doctrine, and questions the idea of truth coming from very broken places. Can truth come from places or people that have distorted the truth, or at least haven't gotten it all right? Of course! God is bigger than the messenger. Does that mean that the messenger is off the hook for their flaws and failures just because God is able to use their mess in some way? The answer is no.

Just as the family I grew up in had problems, as all families do, God still used it in my life. Does that mean that we can ignore problems? No. Paul is pointing to God being bigger than all of this, but there is more to his answer.

Is a Religious Family Any Better Off? (Romans 3:9)

What then? Are we Jews any better off? No, not at all. For we have already charged that all, both Jews and Greeks, are under sin.

Paul gets to the heart of our question now. He asks if the Jews are "any better off." This is very different from asking if there is a benefit. He is asking if their condition apart from Jesus is any different from a non-Jew. This is the equivalent of asking if being born into a Christian family, or into a Christian culture, is enough to make me a Christian. He has said there is a benefit to living within a religious tradition, but it doesn't make their need any different.

Everybody still has sin. Everybody is still in need of salvation through Jesus. No matter if they're born Jewish or if they're born Roman or Greek. In our context, it doesn't matter if we're born white or black, or male or female, rich or poor. Everyone needs Jesus. There is a level playing field, and that doesn't contradict the idea that it's a positive attribute to be born into a family who follows God, or a family who worships Jesus. But does this mean that everyone begins as a "good person"? Let's read a longer passage to answer this question.

Paul's Indictment of All Humanity (Romans 3:10–18)

> As it is written: "None is righteous, no, not one; no one understands; no one seeks for God. All have turned aside; together they have become worthless; no one does good, not even one." "Their throat is an open grave; they use their tongues to deceive." "The venom of asps is under their lips." "Their mouth is full of curses and bitterness." "Their feet are swift to shed blood; in their paths are ruin and misery, and the way of peace they have not known." "There is no fear of God before their eyes."

This is a dire indictment of all humanity. Paul is quoting roughly 27 verses from the Old Testament. For those not familiar with the Bible, the Old Testament is the first two-thirds of the Bible in which is written God's creation of humanity and design for our lives, the condition of humanity in sin, how it happens, and the impact sin has on us today. Paul compiles these verses about the condition of all humanity due to sin to give a picture of our condition apart from Jesus. Recall again from the last chapter the gospel definition motif that we gave—Creation, Fall, Redemption, Restoration. This means that we're caught in the middle—deep in the fall—

between creation and redemption. The fall of Adam sent all of humankind into a tailspin. The first sin had consequences on every human being that would ever be born and that includes you and me. Paul turns everything on its head when we consider questions such as, "Do you have to be a good person to go to heaven?"

As a pastor, I officiate lots of funerals and memorial services. Whether I officiate for a family of faithful Christians, or if I officiate for an unbeliever, there is a common thread of conversation when it comes to the deceased. No one remembers the bad things the deceased have done. They're remembering the best things they did in life. It's common, even in a Christian setting, for them to say, "Oh, I know they're with God, because they were a good person." Believers and unbelievers alike share the same sentiment. Here's the problem. According to Paul, no one's good. No one is seeking God. Human beings were created to live for God, and none of us do. At least, no one does that apart from Jesus transforming his or her life.

Some may object to this line of thinking, but consider this: Have you ever noticed you don't have to teach kids to be selfish? In fact, it's very much the opposite. You have to teach them to share. You don't have to teach a little kid to lie. All you've got to do is catch the child in the middle of doing something he knows is wrong and say, "Did you do this? Did you touch that?" The answer is almost always a guilty "no." Kids will inherently tell a lie just to protect themselves. They will take a toy from another kid and yell, "Mine!" We don't have to teach kids this. We all share this inherent selfishness, and this is the exact opposite of how God created us to be. By design, we are created to give glory to God and love others, not to live selfishly. This is the struggle of every human being.

The truth is, no one is seeking after God. Rather, the opposite is true. God is seeking after people. This realization should stop us in our tracks when we're tempted to use terms like "good" or "bad" in a self-justifying way. When we measure good and bad by the metric of Scripture, we get an entirely different picture. So let's break this down a little bit further by looking at the first few verses Paul uses. That will be enough to gain the point he is getting at.

As it is written: "None is righteous, no, not one" (v. 10)
Paul begins by saying that none of us have right standing with God from our birth. "No, not one." We are all separate from God due to sin. This means that though we may be born into a family of faith, we also need to come into our own faith. Is there a benefit to having a family who follows Jesus? Yes, of course, but only because they are likely to point you to Jesus from a young age. Understanding that no church or family is perfect reminds us that God can use even very broken people and settings to meet us in.

"No one understands; no one seeks for God" (v. 11)
Paul makes a strong statement about no one beginning their life seeking God. This dives into a deeper topic for a different time, but suffice it to say that no one is born with the desire to seek God. In fact, humanity is inherently selfish, or self-seeking. It is God who reaches out to us.

"All have turned aside; together they have become worthless; no one does good, not even one" (v. 12)
Paul makes our point here, and it is the answer to the question we are looking for. *"No one does good, not even one."* What Paul simply states is that no one (apart from the saving

work of Jesus) is good. In other words, there are no good people, "not even one."

Let's frame that into our question. Does God only love good people? The answer, taken from this passage and many others, is that there are no good people. So, indeed, God loves "bad" people. Let's say that in a more user-friendly way: God loves sinful, broken, selfish, corrupt, and undeserving people. That is good news for us, because that is who we are . . . all of us. In the last chapter we referenced Romans 5:8, *"But God shows his love for us in that while we were still sinners, Christ died for us."* It's not bad news to find out that we're bad people, it's part of the gospel message. The gospel is called good news because God loves sinners right where they are. None of us are good, but God is a good God who loves us in our brokenness and failure. Our understanding of our desperate need for Jesus due to the depth of our sin is necessary for us to understand the power of God's gospel to love and change us.

We Are Not Justified by the Law (Romans 3:19–20)

Now we know that whatever the law says it speaks to those who are under the law, so that every mouth may be stopped, and the whole world may be held accountable to God. For by works of the law no human being will be justified in his sight, since through the law comes knowledge of sin.

To be "under the law" means those who live under the rules that God has set out. What it does not mean is that the rules apply to some and not to others. What Paul is getting at is our being "good" based on the rules. I have a sister who is a rule-keeper by nature. I, obviously, am not. We are both followers of Jesus today, but imagine that we are not for a minute. She would still be one who likes to follow rules, and I would not be. What Paul is saying here is that we both need Jesus equally. Following the rules may make you a good citizen, a good employee, or a good driver, but following the rules that God has laid out for us only serves one purpose. It serves to show us that we can't follow them all, and that we are in need of a Savior.

To have God's word, and to possess a template for life (the law), is good. It guides us in understanding God and ourselves. God's law teaches us about our character and our design and how God wants us to live. The problem is, the Scripture also tells us that we're incapable of making ourselves acceptable on our own through law abiding. In Jesus, we see the fulfillment of the Old Testament law, and the fulfillment of the prophets. Not only that, but we also see in Jesus what it looks like to follow God through deep conviction rooted in love, not just living by a written code. Jesus provides an example of love in flesh and blood, human form.

All Have Fallen Short—But Jesus! (Romans 3:21–23)

But now the righteousness of God has been manifested apart from the law, although the Law and the Prophets bear witness to it—the righteousness of God through faith in Jesus Christ for all who believe. For there is no distinction: 'For all have sinned and fall short of the glory of God' and are justified by his grace as a gift, through the redemption that is in Christ Jesus.

The righteousness of God doesn't depend on the family you were born into or the faith that you had before you met Jesus.

55

It also doesn't depend on the lack of faith that you had before you met Jesus. Everybody's on an equal playing field in his or her brokenness. No matter how good a head start you got in life, no matter how amazingly faith-filled your family was, all of us are born broken. All of us are far from God. All of us miss that mark of perfection by choosing ourselves over God. All of us do.

Now, recall the question we want to wrestle with for this chapter: "Does God only love good people?" What about me? Now consider verse 23 and 24 again: *"All have sinned and fall short of the glory of God and are justified by his grace as a gift, through the redemption that is in Christ Jesus."* Often people get stuck on Paul's statement that "all have fallen short." Given the heavy indictment leveled earlier in the chapter, it's easy to get stuck. But we often fail to see the good news if we don't keep reading: we are *"justified by his grace as a gift"* through Jesus!

In later chapters we will unpack in more detail what it means to be justified by God. For now, just know that the hammering all of mankind receives in Romans chapter 3 is meant to get us to the solution: Jesus! None of us can self-justify. None of us are made right by our own efforts, religious heritage, or upbringing alone. There are benefits to getting a head start in life, but it's not enough. All by ourselves, none of us are good. We don't have anything to bring to God in order for Him to accept us. None are inherently good, only Jesus is good. When we believe in what Jesus has done for us, we don't have to self-justify anymore. We are justified through Christ. We don't have to be "good" to be acceptable to God. Rather, Jesus is good for us, in our place.

If you've asked the question, "Does God only love good people?" you're probably asking that because you have a past that has caused you to feel unworthy of God's love. The answer of this chapter should give you great hope. There are no good people. All of humanity is broken and sinful. The great news is that God loves people in the midst of their brokenness. You don't have to earn God's love; He already completely loves you.

WHAT MUST A CHRISTIAN DO TO BE A CHRISTIAN?

Romans 4

What does the Bible say I need to "do" to follow Jesus? Is there a minimum? Are there any requirements? What does it mean to have Jesus as Lord of my life?

I hate running. I often joke that if I'm running, there are police behind me. It's only funny in light of my past, but still makes my point. Consider my perspective. It seems that all my life running was used as punishment. In P.E. class at school, when I got into trouble, I would hear my teacher yell, "Run a lap!" On sports teams when I got into trouble or failed to meet an expectation: "Run a lap!" At Army Boot Camp, as you might guess, I heard the same thing, except with a lot more volume, and an angry sergeant tasked with making a soldier out of me. "Run [what he said next isn't appropriate for print]!" At the time of this writing, I was asked if I would consider running in the Long Beach Marathon. By the way, that date was the third date I had set for that meeting, because

59

I had rescheduled the first two meetings knowing someone would ask me to run. True story.

Believe it or not, I said yes that day and committed to running the half-marathon (13.1 miles). I said yes not because I love running, but for a cause that is greater than my distaste for running. I said yes to run for clean water in Zambia, Africa.[2] I have been to Zambia, and its poorer neighbor Zimbabwe, and have seen the need. I have built friendships with local indigenous pastors there, and I know how important it is for a community to have accessible, clean water.

There is a parable in Matthew in which Jesus tells a story about a King (representing God) thanking His people for caring for Him. He gives examples of people giving Him water, food, and clothes. The people ask the King when they did these things, as they have no recollection of it. Jesus's answer is heart-changing: *"And the King will answer them, 'Truly, I say to you, as you did it to one of the least of these my brothers, you did it to me'"* (Matthew 25:40). Jesus teaches us that when we care for the "least of these," people who are in need on earth, it is equal to doing it in care of God Himself. So, because I have plenty in this life, and others don't even have clean water, I committed to running in spite of my utter hatred of running. I committed to fund raising (asking people to support me by donating to fund clean water), and I trained and ran. October 9th of that year, I ran 13.1 miles. I ran it with friends, teammates from my church and other local churches I am in relationship with, thousands of strangers who acted like family that day, and with a team of close to 300 people

---

2. https://www.worldvision.org/our-work/clean-water.

wearing orange jerseys like mine who had raised money for clean water all over the continent of Africa. I did it for clean water, but honestly, I did it for Jesus and His love for those who don't have what I do.

What Is Actually Required to Become a Christian?

I've been to churches that require that you dress a certain way, and to others that are relaxed about attire. I have been to some churches that require studying a certain translation of the Bible or singing certain songs like psalms and hymns. Some require standing or sitting as a part of their service. Some forms of Christianity require that you only be baptized once, and then some seem to allow it more than once. Even others talk about a baptism in water, and others baptism in the Spirit. Generally speaking, most give a biblical reason for what they do. As a new Christian, I had questions about what Christianity really requires.

"What must a Christian *do* to be a Christian?" For most Christians the solution may sound more simple than it really is. It sounds easy to ask, "What does the Bible say?" But that's simplistic. Part of the problem is that everyone has an "easy" answer. Some Christians attempt to make a tough question into a simple question by saying, "What does the Bible say you are to do?" But that can make it even more complicated. The Bible is a collection of over 60 different writings, across a spectrum of genres, and takes a lot to comprehend. With this complexity in mind, what difficult texts are in the Bible that offer seemingly contradictory answers? Here are three examples:

Because, if you confess with your mouth that Jesus is Lord and believe in your heart that God raised him from the dead, you will be saved.

—Romans 10:9

According to this text, to be a Christian you must "confess that Jesus is Lord" and "believe" in the resurrection, that you are "saved." In this context, "saved" simply means being a Christian saved from the penalty of sin. Does this mean that all someone has to do is believe certain truths about Jesus and tell others about it? Or is there more to being a Christian? What if someone does this, but his life doesn't look Christ-like. Does that matter? Let's look at another verse:

And Peter said to them, "Repent and be baptized every one of you in the name of Jesus Christ for the forgiveness of your sins, and you will receive the gift of the Holy Spirit."

—Acts 2:38

Peter is proclaiming the gospel when the hearers ask him, "What shall we do?" (v. 37). They are asking what they must *do* to be saved (same context of "saved" as above). His answer is very active. Peter, states people need to "repent" and to be "baptized." *Repent* is a word derived from an old military term meaning to turn a full 180 degrees and run for your life. Peter uses this term in a spiritual sense, that people who come to faith in Jesus are required to "turn" from their former way of living and run toward God. He includes baptism, a practice and tradition of being identified with Jesus, and there is a promise of the Holy Spirit that comes through all this.

Do Peter's words contradict Paul's words? Is being a Christian about a confession of faith or the promises of the Holy Spirit and forgiveness? Are these things separate? Let's look at one last passage:

> *But someone will say, "You have faith and I have works."* *Show me your faith apart from your works, and I* *will show you my faith by my works. You believe that* *God is one; you do well. Even the demons believe—and* *shudder!*

> —James 2:18–19

James, a relative of Jesus, writes something entirely different. What James says seems to directly contradict the words of Paul. James says that belief is not enough. Even a demon might believe in the things that Paul says—and is afraid of those things! James says that actions or "works" are required of the Christian. Does that mean a Christian has to work for salvation? That seems contradictory to what Paul teaches. Do these passages contradict one another, or with further study will we find that they say some of the same things from a different perspective? It can be frustrating to think the Bible would leave us so confused.

You have Paul, the most prolific author and leader in the first century church, Peter who was one of Jesus's closest friends and disciples while Jesus was on earth, and James the half brother of Jesus (son of Mary and Joseph), who all give seemingly different answers. Or are they different at all? In the first chapter of this book, we talked about the natural outcome of loving Jesus being a transformed life, so we already know that if we look through the lens of loving Jesus, our actions will follow. However, when we press into the question, "What must I do to be a Christian?" the answer can be a bit murky. Let's unpack this through this letter from Paul that we are reading.

Paul Highlights What "Faith" Means through the Story of Abraham (Romans 12:1-2)

What then shall we say was gained by Abraham, our forefather according to the flesh? For if Abraham was justified by works, he has something to boast about, but not before God.

Who is Abraham, and why is someone who lived almost four thousand years ago important enough for Paul to write about? And, more relevant to us, why is Abraham important today? In a time when people were wandering away from God roughly 3,800 years ago, Abraham (named Abram at that time) was called by God to become a man of faith by leaving who he had been to become someone new. His first big challenge was literally leaving his home, family, and life in general behind, and going to a place God would show him at a future date. Here's the Genesis account of Abram's call:

Now the Lord said to Abram, "Go from your country and your kindred and your father's house to the land that I will show you. And I will make of you a great nation, and I will bless you and make your name great, so that you will be a blessing. I will bless those who bless you, and him who dishonors you I will curse, and in you all the families of the earth shall be blessed." So Abram went, as the Lord had told him.

—Genesis 12:1-4a

Here God calls Abram to leave behind everything he knows, to follow Him so that he can bless others with what he has been given by God. God doesn't even tell Abram where to go, but simply says, "Follow me." God doesn't give Abram a destination, but asks him to trust. Now imagine what that might be like if God said that to you today. How does this relate to the church in Rome?

Remember, the Roman church was a group of brand new Christians who didn't have the religious traditions of the Jewish people. Remember the Judaizers? They came to the Roman church and began teaching that to be a good Christian meant you first had to be a good Jew (you had to *do* something, according to them). Now consider our own context and time. What do we need to *do* to be good Christians? Do we need to wear our Sunday best to the church service? Do we get sprinkled with water or go under the water in baptism? Are we only allowed to sing certain hymns at church? What are we supposed to do with the supposed "rules" that varying Christian traditions hand down? Even more, what do we do with verses that on the surface of things seem to contradict? Let's look in more depth at a few verses. First we'll consider verse 2 before we go on to verse 3. Paul writes in verse 2, *"For if Abraham was justified by works, he has something to boast about, but not before God."*

Faith Counted as Righteousness (Romans 4:3)

Abraham believed God, and it was counted to him as righteousness.

Paul directly contrasts the issue of being justified by works (actions) versus by faith (something more internal). Romans

4:3 is a direct quote from Genesis 15:6. In light of this passage, consider our chapter question again: "What do I have to *do* to be Christian?" Are there things we have to do and rules to keep? Are there things to give up? In Abraham's case, all he did was believe. He believed that the one who was speaking to him was God, and he believed what God called him to was true. But, to be clear, God also called him to *go* somewhere.

In our time and context, we are also called to believe *and* follow Jesus. Paul says this later on in Romans 10:9 by saying, *"If you confess with your mouth that Jesus is Lord and believe in your heart that God raised him from the dead, you will be saved."* What do we have to do to be a Christian? First, we believe Jesus is Lord (note the use of a term that gives headship and authority to our lives). We believe "in our hearts" that God raised Jesus from the dead. In an earlier chapter we talked about the resurrection of Jesus being the proof that He was who He proclaimed Himself to be. Believing that God raised Jesus from the dead also means believing that God has placed a stamp of power and authority on Jesus like no other. To "believe in your heart" is to believe so deeply that the natural outcome is action.

Gifts and Wages (Romans 4:4)

Now to the one who works, his wages are not counted as a gift but as his due. And to the one who does not work, but believes in him who justifies the ungodly, his faith is counted as righteousness.

Within the context of the Roman church, people were saying that believing in Jesus was not enough. They were saying you can believe that Jesus is God, lived a sinless life, died a vicarious death, and rose from the grave, and not be a Christian. But some within the Roman church were proposing there's something you have to do. And this primarily concerned becoming more "Jewish." Paul is writing to this specifically when he says that if a worker goes out, does his job, and gets paid, his pay is not a gift but rather what he's owed.

On the other hand, Paul says salvation is a *gift* from God, not a wage. We're all undeserving. God doesn't owe us forgiveness, mercy, or salvation. But He loves us and gives us the gift of salvation anyway. That's grace. When we're given something that is not ours, all we can do is receive it by faith. By faith, that deep belief in our heart that causes us to be transformed, we get the righteousness of Jesus. We get to be made new, and we're given salvation, paid for by Christ's blood. Now, if we say we deserve salvation because of the things we have *done*, we are really saying that God owes us because we have worked for it, meaning it is not a gift at all.

Righteousness apart from Works (Romans 4:6–8)

Just as David also speaks of the blessing of the one to whom God counts righteousness apart from works: "Blessed are those whose lawless deeds are forgiven, and whose sins are covered; blessed is the man against whom the Lord will not count his sin."

David was king of Israel when Israel was at its height in history. He and his son Solomon led the people of God when Israel was the most powerful nation on the planet. David started as a young man who loved God deeply. But David committed some grievous sins. He cheated on his wife with another man's wife. Driven by guilt and shame, David had the other man murdered. Eventually, David came to terms with all he had done wrong, and he was a deeply broken man because of his sins. When David says, *"Blessed is the man when the Lord does not hold his sins against him,"* we have to understand David was speaking from experience, not theory.

The Bible says those who are forgiven much love much (Luke 7:47). This verse has always resonated with me because my starting point was so bad. When you come to faith in a jail cell as you're waiting to go back to prison, your starting point is bad. My sins were great and grievous. They were done on purpose and were deep. God gave me the greatest gifts in the world—forgiveness and love. In response, I've become grateful. Whatever your experience in life, all our sins are equally great. We're called to reflect on how far from God we can get and that, like David, we say we're blessed because God in His grace has forgiven us. But we know that we have not earned this grace; it is a free gift.

Consider again those three verses we began with from Paul, Peter, and James. Are they contradictory, or do they work together in harmony? I believe these verses are harmonious. But if that's correct, they must either show us important points of the same thing, or they cannot all be true.

Old Testament Signs of Faith (Romans 4:9–10)

Is this blessing then only for the circumcised, or also for the uncircumcised? For we say that faith was counted to Abraham as righteousness. How then was it counted to him? Was it before or after he had been circumcised? It was not after, but before he was circumcised.

If you're unfamiliar with the Bible, the topic of circumcision is likely new territory for you. Circumcision for the Jews was a religious ritual and covenant symbol by which God called the people of God to make a profession of faith. Here's the question: Was Abraham considered righteous before or after his circumcision? Did God "bless" Abraham because he did something physical and tangible to earn God's love, or was Abraham blessed simply because he had faith in God?

When God calls Abraham to follow Him, he does. Righteousness is then credited to Abraham due to the faith he had in God which was shown in how he did what God called him to do. That was how Abraham was "counted righteous." Then, while doing what God had called him to do, Abraham receives the covenant symbol of circumcision and acts on it. He again was considered righteous by God through his faith, which was shown again in his actions. It was not after Abraham did things God told him to, but before that God considered him faithful.

Let's put it in a modern-day context, swapping baptism for circumcision, and say that Abraham is a Christian who has not been baptized. God already loves him and sees him as perfect, which is why God strikes up a conversation with Abraham. Then God says, "I want to make a covenant with you. Through your family, Abraham, I'm going to bring Jesus, and all the families of the earth are going to be blessed. Not just given something nice, but be blessed with eternal salvation." Now if God said this blessing would come through Abraham, and the sign would be baptism, our question now is, "Does baptism make one righteous, or is baptism something followers of Jesus do in response and obedience?" According to Paul's example, it is in response and obedience. Likewise, when the people in Jerusalem ask Peter what they must "do" to be saved, his answer is to "repent and be baptized." Why is his answer an action step? Because the action is proof of the belief and faith in God, not a work that merits the love of God.

Fast forward to the Roman church. Roman Christians, like those in Acts 2 in Jerusalem, began asking, "What do we have to do in order to be Christian?" At that time, Judaizers were claiming that all the men in the church had to undergo circumcision. Paul wrote about this issue and reminded them that you can't add to the gospel of grace. You can't add to the salvation that Jesus accomplished with His life, death, and resurrection. For Paul, salvation comes by confessing with your mouth, believing that Jesus came, lived, died, and rose again for our sin. That's it. He would clearly say that those things will result in actions but not be predicated on them.

What Do We Do with Baptism and Peter's Answer?

Baptism is a response in obedience and faith to what Jesus has already done inside us. Those who are baptized are taking steps of faith (obedience), in line with their repentance (leaving their disobedience), and believing that God will fill them with the promised Holy Spirit. We do the same. Peter is right when he says, "Repent and be baptized." We need to turn from any false beliefs that we work for our salvation and start pointing our heart and mind toward Jesus. Our first step in that direction is baptism.

Now, why do we equate baptism with circumcision? Paul makes this connection for us in Colossians 2.

The Example of Baptism versus Circumcision

Since Paul uses the example of circumcision with Abraham throughout several verses, and Peter is calling all Christians to be baptized, it is important for us to do a little work on why we tie those two together. It is easy to see when we look at another letter that Paul wrote to another church in a city called Colossae. Paul tells them in Colossians 2:11–12:

> *In him also you were circumcised with a circumcision made without hands, by putting off the body of the flesh, by the circumcision of Christ, having been buried with him in baptism, in which you were also raised with him through faith in the powerful working of God, who raised him from the dead.*

Paul says to the Church in Colossae, to both men and women, you were also circumcised, regardless of your gender or physical state, with a circumcision not made with hands. There's no blood involved in this circumcision. You were circumcised by a cutting away of your "flesh" when you were baptized in Christ's name. When you went into the water, you died to the flesh, and when you came out of the water you were raised in Christ's victorious resurrection (more on this in the coming chapter covering Romans 6). The New Testament covenant symbol is baptism, not circumcision. The reason for a new covenant symbol, for what is actually very much the fulfillment of the same promise God made to Abraham, is the removal of anything causing blood. While God's covenant with Abraham is everlasting, there can be no longer a covenant symbol still made with blood because Jesus satisfied the covenant with His own blood. That means

71

we no longer need circumcision. We identify with Christ in baptism.

Baptism, Circumcision, and Passover

Because this is often tough to follow, let's look at the easier-to-see Old Testament covenant symbol fulfilled in the New Testament by Jesus, where the church is given a new covenant symbol to participate in. No Christian that I know today believes we are required to observe Passover each year by slaughtering a lamb and having a meal together. That was an Old Testament covenant symbol that has been replaced by Communion. Jesus makes a profound statement over the cup during that meal, by saying, "This cup that is poured out for you is the new covenant in my blood" (Luke 22:20). In the same way, Paul teaches us that because of Christ's blood satisfying all need for blood, the new symbol is baptism, a covenant symbol showing how God has passed over our sin and brokenness because of Jesus.

But the same question exists: Do we have to be baptized to be a Christian? If baptism replaced circumcision as the sign of being in covenant with God, does that mean we have to do it? Like Paul, we can point to Abraham and note that baptism is an obedient response to placing our faith in Jesus. Baptism shows our faith, but it doesn't accomplish it. It may validate that we have a genuine faith, but it does not create it.

But the more familiar you get with your Bible, the more questions may arise. In Acts 2 Peter is asked what people should do to be saved. He explains, *"Repent and be baptized, every one of you, in the name of Jesus Christ for the forgiveness of your sins, and you will receive the gift of the Holy Spirit"* (v. 38). What Peter says doesn't add to salvation. When God has begun doing something in your heart and you come to faith, you respond by identifying with the covenant symbol of baptism. You have a change of mind and turn the opposite way. The shorthand way of saying this is that you repent. Your mind changes the way you lived in the past, and you begin to identify with Christ. When you go under the water of baptism, God meets you there. He pours out grace on you and gives you His Spirit. So you see, we don't have to do anything to earn our salvation. We do something in response to receiving salvation.

The Footsteps of Faith (Romans 4:11–12)

He received the sign of circumcision as a seal of the righteousness that he had by faith while he was still uncircumcised. The purpose was to make him the father of all who believe without being circumcised, so that righteousness would be counted to them as well, and to make him the father of the circumcised who are not merely circumcised but who also walk in the footsteps of the faith that our father Abraham had before he was circumcised.

Here's how this all comes full circle: Paul writes that Abraham was righteous *before* he was circumcised. Abraham went through circumcision as a *response* to his faith because he was accepted and by loved God. We do the same thing. We turn and identify with Jesus, and we're baptized as a form of obedience to our faith. Jesus fulfilled the literal need to cut away a part of the flesh. Because we have died to the flesh, we come out of the water of baptism and arise in Christ. Abraham was circumcised as the first among many who would later be baptized into the faith. We walk in the footsteps of his faith.

This flow from faith to action is not contradictory. When we repent, our values and lives change. They begin to mirror those of our Lord and Savior Jesus. We begin to love the same things that Jesus loves and care for the same things that Jesus cares for. We walk away from the things that Jesus walked away from. He empowers us to live like Him. While we'll never be perfect or even get close, we reflect the sentiment of James 2:19 by showing our faith by our works.

Again, here's how the Apostle James speaks about living in faith in James 2:18–19: *"Someone will say, you have faith and I have works. You show me your faith apart from your works, and I will show you my faith by my works."* In effect, James says, "I'm going to show you how I love Jesus because Jesus has changed my life. You say you have faith that is apart from works. That's true and good. But faith can never be void of works, change, or obedience. That kind of faith can never stand." As Christians, we have to hold this tension. Our obedience is never grounds for our salvation. In fact, if we approach our Christian life that way, Paul says our faith is *"null and void"* (see below). Our faith is enough, yet it produces action.

God's Promises Come through Faith, Not Obedience (Romans 4:13–14)

> *For the promise to Abraham and his offspring that he would be heir of the world did not come through the law but through the righteousness of faith. For if it is the adherents of the law who are to be the heirs, faith is null and the promise is void.*

If salvation comes to us through obeying the law, we're never going to make it because none of us are able to obey perfectly. Paul explains it this way in his letter to the Ephesians: *"For we're saved by grace through faith and this is not of your own doing, it is the gift of God. It is not the result of works so that no one may boast. For we're his workmanship created in Christ Jesus for good works, which God prepared beforehand that we should walk in them."* We're saved by faith, not by anything we do on our own. It is through grace that we stand before God and even have the faith to believe, because God has given us the faith to believe. In every step of faith we take, God strengthens us. When we respond in baptism, God pours out his Spirit, and our hearts and minds begin to change. Faith snowballs in the right direction as we become more and more conformed to the image of Christ over a lifetime.

How Should We Respond?

We opened this book, asking the question, "Is loving Jesus enough?" Yes, it absolutely is enough to love Jesus. And loving Jesus causes us to live differently. Jesus says, "If you love me, you'll obey my commandments." He doesn't say, "Obey my commandments and prove you love me." He says that if we love Him, the natural outpouring in day-to-day life is that we're going to change, be different people. The more we love Jesus, the more we begin to look like our Savior. But we have to be on guard and not believe it's our obedience to God's law that makes us acceptable before God.

Let's walk out how to live each of the three verses in our lives today. If you've never given your life to following Jesus, do so today. Even if these concepts seem foreign, take the first step of faith. Think about Abram, to whom God said, "I want you to leave everything, and I want you to go." Leaving a life behind and taking that step of faith had to be the hardest thing

Abram had ever done. But God is faithful, and He met him in that first step. God does the same for us. He joins us and gives us the strength for the next step, and the next.

If you're a follower of Jesus, receive His gift of grace. Become part of a church and be baptized. Then, play an active role in faith. We're not called to sit on the side-lines and say our own personal belief is enough. We don't earn salvation. Good works are not enough. We respond in faith because we already have favor with God, and we want to make an impact in the world out of our gratitude for God.

WHY AM I SO BROKEN?

Romans 5

When we consider our broken world and the sin and suffering we endure, we inevitably have to ask ourselves, "Why are things as they are?"

As a pastor, my time is often spent talking to people who feel broken inside. Some are painfully depressed, some are hopelessly addicted to drugs, spending, pornography, or drinking. Some are attracted to same-sex relationships and don't want to be, and there are others who struggle with illness and health issues. This is not an all-encompassing list of the sufferings, but they're common.

When we consider our broken world and the sin and suffering we endure, we inevitably have to ask ourselves, "Why are things as they are? Why do our loved ones suffer? Why do we each continue to struggle with sin in our life?" To put it simply: the world is broken. So am I, and so are you. Why though? I understand this personally today as well as in the past. I remember feeling unable to change my life when I was addicted to drugs. I spent about fifteen years so dependent on meth-amphetamines that I couldn't get out of bed without them and couldn't stop using them even though they were killing me.

Finding Peace (Romans 5:1–2)

Therefore, since we have been justified by faith, we have peace with God through our Lord Jesus Christ. Through him [Jesus] we have also obtained access by faith into this grace in which we stand, and we rejoice in hope of the glory of God.

Whenever we see the word *therefore* in a biblical text, it is important to understand what it is pointing to. In this case, it is Paul signaling that the point he is about to make is built on an understanding of the justification that he has already covered. Justification is only common today as a biblical term, but not really anywhere else. Here's something that might help us understand: Imagine for a moment your personal finances. Most of us have felt overwhelmed by debt. Imagine being so deep in debt that you don't know how to get out of it. In accounting, the phrase "to be justified" means the removal of the debt, the balancing of your finances. Paul is using the image of indebtedness so that we see our sin as having caused a great debt to God. However, by placing our faith in Jesus and the payment He has made on our behalf by dying in our place, our debt has been "justified" or paid in full. Building on this, Paul takes the next step.

Now, in this justification through Jesus paying our debt, we have peace with God and access to Him. Let's unpack a few pieces of what Paul is getting at. There are two side-by-side images that work together and have complementary meanings. Having a debt that is paid results in peace, because we had been in bondage due to this debt. Receiving peace implies that we didn't have peace in the past, and in fact we were at war with God. The war is that we are in rebellion to God by choosing our way over God's way, and that causes us to be indebted to God. Through Jesus and His accomplishment on the cross, our debt to God of sin has been paid by Jesus, and in the resurrection of Christ where we have obtained new life, we are now reconciled and no longer at odds with God.

Now, because of this, we have peace—not only peace with God, but peace in this life. Here is where we can press into this chapter. If we have peace, how can it be that we feel so broken? That is a great way to address this topic.

First, let's finish what Paul is talking about here. When we place our lives into Jesus's hands, we get access to everything we need. What we need is God's grace. But what is the content of that grace? Jesus was fully divine and fully human. In His love for us, He endured all that we go through in this life. Not only did He endure a human life, He lived sinlessly to overcome our struggles. For every bad decision I've made, Jesus made correct decisions. He took our sin to the cross, died for it, and paid our penalty. In His resurrection, He gives us new life. You and I inherited a victorious life when Jesus rose from death. Now the ascended Jesus pours out His spirit on all those who trust in Him so that we're empowered to live at peace in this life as we eagerly wait in anticipation for His return.

When Paul writes that we have *obtained access into this grace*" (v. 2), he's saying we have full access to what Christ has accomplished for us and given to us. The challenge for us today is learning how to live in light of that. Paul gives us an image of learning to stand in grace. This means that we learn to live in light of this grace everyday.

One problem that we have is that we often believe that by coming to faith in Jesus, immediately life will become pain free. But that isn't necessarily true. It still takes grace to live every day. In this broken world, we will still have struggles. As Jesus says in John 16:33, "*In the world you will have tribulation* [and brokenness]. *But take heart; I have overcome the world.*" We're going to struggle in this life, but we have everything we need to grow, heal, and flourish by standing in the grace of Jesus.

Our Hope in Suffering (Romans 5:3–5)

> *Not only that, but we rejoice in our sufferings, knowing that suffering produces endurance, and endurance produces character, and character produces hope, and hope does not put us to shame, because God's love has been poured into our hearts through the Holy Spirit who has been given to us.*

What comes next is a surprise. Paul tells us that "*we rejoice in our sufferings*" and that suffering produces in us endurance, character, and hope. But what does this mean? Is it a bumper-sticker solution to real-life problems? Is this Paul trying to give us a Twitter-sized solution? Paul, who is considered by many to be the greatest Christian second only to Jesus, seemed to have it together. But notice that Paul is using language that includes himself. What he's saying is that *we* suffer and *we* struggle and *we all* face challenges in this life. Paul is saying that life isn't always the way he would like it, but he rejoices in suffering.

This isn't a simple, bumper-sticker solution or platitude to life. According to Paul, suffering and brokenness can truly produce positive change in us, do not have to cause shame in us, and are bearable with God's love and Spirit in us. Suffering or brokenness produces feelings in us that there's something we're unable to fix or change, or at least do so easily. But suffering can produce Christ-like attributes in us. Listen to how Paul develops this: "*Our suffering produces endurance, and endurance produces character. Character gives us hope, and hope will not put us to shame.*" Our brokenness doesn't have to bring us shame. Instead it can be useful in growing us spiritually.

Most of us feel that whatever struggle we have is negative, that we're alone, that we can't talk about struggles in public places, struggles such as mental illness, sexuality, or finances. These kinds of struggles can cause us to feel isolated and shameful. But what if we shared all of our ugly stuff with loving, trustworthy people? What if everyone in the church laid it all out there and were honest? If we could do so—and not gossip—we'd realize that what is in us is also in all of us.

Just recently I had a friend take me to the airport. On our drive, I mentioned that sometimes I struggle with feeling guilty about my past. When my thoughts get the best of me, I think that today's problems must be a penalty for my past. I know that's not true, but it doesn't always take away the feeling. These feelings are rare, but they still come. My friend said that my willingness to share my own brokenness and anxieties helped him know that he's not alone.

We're not alone in this life. We don't have to be ashamed of our pain due to sin and suffering. I don't have to approve of my struggles, but I don't have to be ashamed of them anymore either. Everyone in the church is messed up, together. We can have hope that life is bearable with God's love and Spirit in us. God knows the brokenness and the pain better than we do, yet He still loves us. His Spirit is in us. He knows all the ugly parts of us, and still He loves us.

Christ Died for the Ungodly (Romans 5:6–8)

For while we were still weak, at the right time Christ died for the ungodly. For one will scarcely die for a righteous person—though perhaps for a good person one would dare even to die—but God shows his love for us in that while we were still sinners, Christ died for us.

There is a myth in Christianity that you have to clean yourself up to be presentable to God. Remember in chapter 3 we talked about the myth of thinking we're good people. This is Paul developing this idea further, saying that we're broken and messed up people, yet God still loves us. In verse 8, he says, *"While we were still sinners Christ died for us."* We don't come to God all fixed up. No, when we were still indebted to God in sin and separated from Him, Jesus died for us. But there's a pervading belief that we have to change in order to go to church. It tells us things like, "I can't go to church because I'm still strung out on heroin," or, "I can't go to church because I'm in the midst of a divorce." But Paul tells us that when we were in the middle of those sorts of problems and sin, that's when Jesus gave His life for us. It's while we're at our worst, while we're at our neediest, while we're at our most broken that the love of God is poured out to us through His Son.

I've shared much of my story, and these verses definitely

apply to me. When I came to faith in Jesus, I was a deeply broken person. How could I have possibly fixed myself up and come to God in that state? I couldn't; that was the whole point. God met me in my brokenness, while I was still weak. Christ came and died for you and for me—the ungodly.

What Does Paul Mean by "Much More" (Romans 5:9-11)

Since, therefore, we have now been justified by his blood, much more shall we be saved by him from the wrath of God. For if while we were enemies we were reconciled to God by the death of his Son, much more, now that we are reconciled, shall we be saved by his life. More than that, we also rejoice in God through our Lord Jesus Christ, through whom we have now received reconciliation.

A few chapters ago, we dealt with the wrath of God. This is not something spoken about much in most churches. But if we don't understand the wrath of God, we don't understand what we are saved from. Thankfully, God justifies us through Christ. Here is another contrasting word that we would do well to pay attention to: *reconciled.* Think back to earlier in this chapter about how we are now at peace with God on account of Jesus. The implication of establishing peace is that we did not have peace with God at one time.

In fact, Paul uses the language of our being "enemies" with God. In our culture, there's a tendency to believe that everybody is a good person and that we all really strive to be good people. But that's not accurate. The picture that the

Bible gives is that we are people running passionately away from God and into sin. But God, in His love, pursues us. We're made to live in relationship with God. To be loved by Him and to love others. Instead, we choose lesser things for our lives and make our lives all about us. To be in opposition to God makes us enemies of God.

But Paul says in verse 10, *"If while we were enemies we were reconciled to God by the death of his Son, much more, now that we are reconciled, shall we be saved by his life."* Do you see? Everything that was lost because of the Fall and our own rebelliousness has been given back to us. We can be sure of this because of how Paul describes our reconciliation with God. Notice the bolded words in the following verses. Verse 9 says, *"**Much more** shall we be saved by him from the wrath of God."* Then in verse 10, *"**Much more**, now that we are reconciled, shall we be saved by his life."* And then in verse 11 Paul highlights the point again: *"**More than that**, we also rejoice in God through our Lord Jesus Christ, through whom we have now received reconciliation."*

Paul's aim is to show our redemption and restoration. Remember the "Creation, Fall, Redemption, and Restoration" motif from a few chapters ago? This section of Scripture lays it all out beautifully. God pays our debt, but He's not just covering over our past sins. He's doing so much more. Paul is talking about God entering into our present-tense suffering and brokenness and redeeming our lives in the here and now. God is actively recreating us to reflect our intended design as whole human beings. In Jesus, we've been reconciled, and we are *being* reconciled. What Jesus began for you will be seen through to its completion.

Why Is There So Much Brokenness in This Life? (Romans 5:12)

Therefore, just as sin came into the world through one man, and death through sin, and so death spread to all men because all sinned.

In order to fully understand Paul's arguments, we have to do some work in understanding certain doctrines. In Romans 5:12, we get to the doctrine of Adamic sin—meaning the sin that we inherited from Adam.

Here's a way to think about it: Imagine growing up with parents who smoked in the house, and their parents before them smoked in the house. When you were born, before you ever had a chance to smoke yourself, you got smoke in your lungs even if you didn't ask for it. There is a high chance that you're going to suffer consequences. Now imagine you smoke for 40 years and then decide to quit. Do all the problems go away immediately? Might they ever?

This is a picture of Adamic sin. We are inheriting the guilt of thousands of generations of human beings. We've chosen to participate in that guilt as well. None of us are perfect. None of us are without having done something wrong, knowing it was wrong. We all know that we are inheritors of this guilt and are contributors to it. It's no wonder our world is broken. It's no wonder our lives don't look the way that Jesus created them to look. It's no wonder that we struggle.

Whether or not you become a nonsmoker, all your inherited history, and the history you contributed to, stays with you. You might still struggle to breathe. Human brokenness and the result of Adamic sin is so heavy that sometimes you feel as if you can't breathe. It begins to make sense when we recognize that we both inherit and contribute to this guilt.

Here it is again: *"Therefore just as sin came into the world through one man and death through sin so death spread to all men because all sinned."* This is the reason why humanity is so broken. We're born under a death caused by the sins of all humanity throughout history. This is not the world God created but the one that has been destroyed by sin—a world of sin we have participated in. It is incredibly important that we understand both our inherited guilt and our own contribution. We have a starting point that's corrupt, and then we add to it. This is the doctrine of Adamic sin in a nutshell.

Our Inheritance in Adam and in Jesus (Romans 5:13–14)

> *For sin indeed was in the world before the law was given, but sin is not counted where there is no law. Yet death reigned from Adam to Moses, even over those whose sinning was not like the transgression of Adam, who was a type of the one who was to come.*

Paul calls Adam a "type," or foreshadowing, of Jesus. Adam gave us an inheritance of one kind (sin, death, and brokenness). Christ gives us another inheritance (redemption, forgiveness, and life). Adam had a huge impact on all of history. He misled people, and the inheritance was the pain and struggle we have today. Christ, the second Adam, gives us a new inheritance— the inheritance of blessing we were intended to have.

This demonstrates the depth of God's love. He didn't have to come and give us a second inheritance. By inheritance and through our own guilt we own the first. By grace we are saved through faith in Jesus. Now that we feel the weight of our problem, let's look into the solution.

Humanity Has Big Problems, but Jesus Is a Bigger Solution (Romans 5:15–17)

But the free gift is not like the trespass. For if many died through one man's trespass, much more have the grace of God and the free gift by the grace of that one man Jesus Christ abounded for many. And the free gift is not like the result of that one man's sin. For the judgment following one trespass brought condemnation, but the free gift following many trespasses brought justification. For if, because of one man's trespass, death reigned through that one man, much more will those who receive the abundance of grace and the free gift of righteousness reign in life through the one man Jesus Christ.

Jesus is our second Adam—the right, the greater, the better Adam—and as adopted children, we inherit the best. The inheritance we get in Jesus allows us to move from condemnation to justification. As was previously said, the debt of our sin is condemnation, but Jesus has set us free from that debt burden. We can either pay the penalty for our own sin in condemnation and judgment, or we can be set free from inherited guilt and the guilt we incur on ourselves. That's justification and salvation. That's the free gift of a loving God who gave his Son for us. Christians have been given something new, not just the removal of sin, brokenness, and pain, but a restored relationship with God. We've been turned from enemies to sons and daughters of God. We're not only forgiven, but we are being transformed and restored in Jesus.

As big as the problem is, the solution is so *much* bigger. Again, Paul is using the language "much more" in verses 15 and 17. His point is that what we inherited in Christ is much more than what we inherited in Adam. What that means for us today is that our redemption in Jesus is greater than our brokenness in Adam. This means we have the hope of overcoming the things in this life that plague us so much.

Why would Paul spend so much time on the ugliness of our debt of sin? Here's an answer and a point to take away: We inherited this ugly, painful internal war within us. Instead of making it better, we added to it. But now in Christ, we inherit the victory and blessing of Jesus. Remember, we've obtained access to the grace in which we stand, the grace that is needed for us to live every day, to take every breath, to get up out of bed and go to work, to go to church, to stay married, to raise kids, to overcome brokenness, and to do anything God has called us to do.

So many times people hear the gospel. Often it's told with one of two different outcomes. One is that our sin is forgiven, and the second is that we go to heaven when we die. But the pain of living in a broken world is still with us. It's not *just* that we get forgiveness and eternity. It's that *today* God wants to reconcile our brokenness in the here and now.

We've ended this chapter on a dark note. But just know that in a few chapters we're going to get to some hopeful themes. In chapter 7, we're going to talk about how the victory of Christ applies to us. When we consider our chapter question, "Why am I so broken?" Paul leads us to an answer we might not want to hear. We're so broken because we've lived with millennia of sin and because we've contributed to that sin ourselves. Living with that can feel dark and depressing. That's a heavy burden to bear. But Paul can't leave us there. Ultimately Paul leaves us with an encouraging message: though our sin and debt to God is great, the hope of Jesus is much bigger than the problem, and a key to that hope is that we are being sanctified.

Sanctification is a word the Bible unpacks time and time again. The simple definition of sanctification is that we're being conformed into the image of Jesus. What Paul says is that, though we are born under Adam's image in brokenness and sin, we are being reborn into the image of Jesus. Jesus is healing the worst and most painful pieces of our lives, and that takes a long time. Understanding the problem (sin) helps us learn how to live into the solution (Jesus). We will be unpacking this in upcoming chapters. For now, we can know our solution is much bigger than the problem.

ARE ALL CHRISTIANS HYPOCRITES?

Romans 6

How do we as followers of Jesus deal with the reality of sin and the calling of holiness in a way that is honest, glorifies Jesus, and isn't hypocritical?

There are times in which I go to church while I'm struggling with something in my life. When asked how I am doing, I keep my struggles a secret. When someone greets me and asks, "How are you," my response *could* be something like, "You know, I'm struggling right now with something." I could be vulnerable and honest.

Admittedly, most people want a simple answer like, "Good, how are you?" But sometimes I hide how I really am doing. Though it may seem small, this kind of masking the truth in small ways can grow into a dual life that ends up being deeply problematic down the line.

In recent years, studies have been done to determine what

unbelievers think about the Christian faith.[3] One common answer is that people believe Christians are hypocrites—that Christians profess something they don't live. They say one thing and do another. With this in mind, let's ask our chapter question again, "Are all Christians hypocrites?" I know Christians often hide their struggles, sometimes thinking that their feelings will be a bad witness for their faith, when in reality they comes across as hypocrites, which is worse. And of course there are people who are living dual lives—everyone knows that's wrong. What we want to consider is how a Christian lives in the tension of being called to live like Jesus and the reality of everyday struggles that everyone faces.

A hypocrite is defined as "one who puts on a false appearance of virtue or religion." It comes from the Greek word *hypokrites*. Hypokrites is believed to have been a person, but for sure we can trace the name back to a man named Thespis. Those who know the world of drama have heard the term *thespian*. Thespis introduced hypokrites, his actors who would wear masks and take on different personas according to the mask he put on. To be a hypocrite, in its simplest understanding, is to be someone who puts on a mask to cover up who they really are.

Christians sometimes "put on masks" to impersonate being different than what they are. Maybe it is acting as they live one way around Christians, and then another way around those who don't have a faith they claim. Or maybe it is just

---

3. https://www.amazon.com/unChristian-Generation-Really-Christianity -Matters/dp/0801072719/ref=sr_1_1?ie=UTF8&qid=1486063336&sr =8-1&keywords=unchristian.

hiding who they really are inside. Some Christians hide their struggles, not wanting to misrepresent Jesus. But it comes across as hypocrisy. All of these examples are detrimental to the image of Christ and the Church, whether the motives are good or bad.

Now, I am not saying that I am a hypocrite just because I didn't share my struggles to some person who asked me a common morning greeting. Rather, I am pointing to the idea of wearing a "mask" covering up who I truly am. Those outside the faith often perceive Christians as hypocrites, because they portray themselves one way and then live another way. They put on masks and try to appear different from who they really are. Maybe we could reframe the question as follows: How do we as followers of Jesus deal with the reality of sin and the calling of holiness, while being honest, glorifying Jesus, and avoiding hypocrisy?

The Reality of Sin in the Christian Life (Romans 6:1-2)

> *What shall we say then? Are we to continue in sin that grace may abound? By no means! How can we who died to sin still live in it.*

The reality is that sin exists in every life, including mine and yours. To live a life of faith means that we are called to live according to the values God has given us. However we are still trapped in the many sinful things we do, which reflect parts of who we are inside that still struggle. Clearly our real life exists in the tension. Those of us who profess to be followers of Jesus are not all bad or entirely consumed by our sin. However, we aren't all good, living lives of perfect obedience to Jesus either. So how do we live in the "in between" without putting on masks to hide from others? We want to grow, mature, and honestly represent Jesus to the rest of the world. This is the tension we live in and wrestle with today.

This is similar to what Paul dealt with in his day. In order to tackle some of these questions, Paul gives us some very practical theology. Theology isn't reserved for academics or seminarians; it's for all of us, especially when approached in a practical way. At the beginning of Romans 6, Paul asks, *"What do we say then? Are we to continue in sin that grace may abound?"* His rhetorical question is good for us to start with. If we are followers of Jesus, are we supposed to continue living the same way we used to—in sin? Does being forgiven mean we don't need to change the way we live?

His question is aimed at a false understanding of forgiveness and holiness. Forgiveness and grace are such a huge part of the gospel message, and if they are not understood correctly they can lead to a very disparate understanding of the nature of our sin and our calling to live in a new way. If continuing in sin is not acceptable, then how can we call ourselves Christians and keep on sinning? Certainly, we can't continue in sin. Paul's answer to his rhetorical question is, *"By no means! How can we who died to sin still live in it?"*

Baptized into Jesus (Romans 6:3–5)

Do you not know that all of us who have been baptized into Christ Jesus were baptized [immersed] into Jesus' death? We were buried therefore with him by baptism into death, in order that, just as Christ was raised from the dead by the glory of the Father, we too might walk in newness of life. For if we have been united with him in a death like his, we shall certainly be united with him in a resurrection like his.

Paul says something surprising. He mentions baptism and Jesus's death. Baptism, going under the water physically, is identification with the death of Jesus, or dying to sin. This is why Paul picks up that theme. He says, "How can we who died to sin still live in sin?" A great question and a tough one to answer. That is because there is a powerful undercurrent to being born in brokenness like we discussed in the previous chapter. No matter how good of a job our moms did raising us, they couldn't raise us to be contrary to human brokenness. What happens when we continue in sin and call ourselves Christian? This is the hypocrisy question that we are dealing with.

The word *baptism* ["baptidzo" in Greek] means to immerse a fabric in a different color, to dye it. When it comes out of the dye, it is a different color. What Paul is saying is that those who have been *immersed* into Christ Jesus were also *immersed* (baptized) into His death. When we emerge from the water, we are now equipped to be different. But how? When believers are baptized, by God applying a means of grace to them, they participate in the death that Jesus died and in His resurrected life. When I baptize people in our church, I use descriptive biblical words for what is happening. They go down into the water, and I say, "Die to the flesh," and when they come up out of the water, I say, "Arise in life." This is because we believe that God truly meets them in that moment, and something real and empowering takes place.

When we're given new life, we're not just left under the water, which would actually cause us to die! However, we go in and come out made new. Not only do we identify with

Jesus's death in baptism, but we also come out of the water identifying with Jesus's resurrection as well. We go in one way, dying to the way we have always lived dominated by our sinful nature; when we come up out of the water, we arise "alive in Christ."

Something real takes place in baptism, and it also shapes our life. Paul says that we're given the ability to begin walking in a new way and become different people. Yet we still live in a broken world, and we still have broken pieces of our lives in us. There's a calling to live in a new way, and there is a promise that we have a new ability to accomplish what God is calling us to. Baptism is the outward image of an inward reality. It isn't the water of baptism that enables us to "walk in newness of life"; it is the death and resurrection of Jesus being applied to us through the Holy Spirit that empowers us. Paul teaches us that we are given a new ability in Christ that we did not have before, an ability to live in a new way.

I don't know if you remember this, but there was a show on TV in the 80s called *The Greatest American Hero*. The main character was a regular guy who suddenly was given superpowers—like the ability to fly—but he didn't know how to use his powers yet and kept crashing into walls in mid-air. Maybe you don't know that reference, but consider this life snapshot from real life. Imagine a kid trying to learn how to ride a bike. One day balance suddenly clicks and he's able to ride his bike, but he's still going to have to learn balance after many hours of practice. Just like a kid learning to ride a bike, we'll fall down and skin our knees. As Christians, we will fail. But over time, we will get better. Learning to walk in this newness of life takes a lifetime.

Baptism is something that Christians are called to do as an act of obedience. More than obedience, baptism is also a means of grace as stated above. There is truly a spiritual implication. God uses these unique moments like baptism to transform us. Paul is asking, "Don't you know that something took place when you were baptized? You died with Christ, and you're now raised with him to new life."

Keep in mind, Paul is writing to a church filled with believers who he probably assumes are baptized. He is reminding them that they are now indwelt with the Spirit of Jesus (Holy Spirit) and empowered to live a new life.

Breaking Free from the Slavery of Sin (Romans 6:6–10)

We know that our old self was crucified with him in order that the body of sin might be brought to nothing, so that we would no longer be enslaved to sin. For one who has died has been set free from sin. Now if we have died with Christ, we believe that we will also live with him. We know that Christ, being raised from the dead, will never die again; death no longer has dominion over him. For the death he died he died to sin, once for all, but the life he lives he lives to God.

Paul is not commending slavery, and he's not saying slavery is OK. He's been misunderstood on this point by some. In fact, he wrote an entire book of the Bible that says he is not pro-slavery. In verse 6, Paul uses an existing reality in the Roman culture to make a point about a spiritual reality that they may not quite understand. He says, "We know that our old self was crucified with him in order that the body of sin might be brought to nothing, so that we would no longer be enslaved to sin."

Very few of us have experienced human slavery. We've read about it in history, and it still exists in some parts of the world. As wrong as slavery is and as ignorant as we may be, we get a picture of what it's like. I can look at my own background, with a long history of drug use, the difficulties endured, and the trouble that came with it, and I can say, I was enslaved to my own sin. I was trapped. I made choices I had to pay for. Maybe you have your own version of being enslaved to sin.

Our current-day context is obviously different from that of the Church in Rome, but there is a thematic tie: all Christians had an old self before meeting Jesus. Apart from Jesus, I was much worse off. Then I met Jesus, and He rescued me and is changing me over time. That doesn't mean that the change was immediate, that the bad decisions I had made went away, and that the prison doors miraculously flew open—I know, because I checked. But I will say this: after many years of my own effort, I couldn't quit drugs. It was God who healed me of drug addiction. Over time I began changing. I could identify my old self and was experiencing transformation. I started thinking in terms of who I was, and I knew there was still a call on my life for who I was supposed to become. I was in between the two worlds. In fact, I'm still there. That old self was crucified with Christ so that it might be brought to nothing. The passage notes that if a slave dies, he or she is no longer enslaved to whatever he or she was enslaved to. They're dead. They're freed.

Dying to sin and death and being raised to new life is something that Jesus does in us and for us, not something we do. Death occurred at the cross, and we were set free from slavery to sin. But we weren't perfected instantaneously. We don't become who we're called to be in a moment. Instead, we're made new and set on a different trajectory. We're given a new ability, by grace, to begin living a new way. Doors open up, and we're given a new power, a new ability, and a new heart. Paul says the old self, who we used to be, is nailed to the cross with Christ. Now the new self is given life by Christ's resurrection, which sets us on a new path. When Jesus died and rose from the grave, something actually took place that impacts us. In verses 9–11, Paul says, *"We know that Christ being raised from the dead will never die again. Death no longer has dominion over him. For the death he died, he died to sin. Once for all, but the life he lives he lives to God. You must also consider yourselves dead to sin and alive to God and Christ Jesus."* If we understand our baptism to be identifying ourselves with those realities, it changes us. Baptism is our outward identification of what God is doing inwardly.

Behavior Follows Belief (Romans 6:11)

So you also must consider yourselves dead to sin and alive to God in Christ Jesus.

If Jesus died for something to change in us, then Jesus also rose from the dead for something to be changed. The Greek word for repentance, *metanoia*, means to have a complete change of mind. Paul is saying we should begin to believe, understand, and live differently. This reminds me of a story about an elephant. Once a man was walking by a large elephant only tied down by a small rope. So he asked the elephant trainer, "How is such a massive creature held down by a tiny rope?" Here was the trainer's reply: "Well, when they are very young and much smaller we use the same size of rope to tie them and, at that age, it's enough to hold them. As they grow up, they are conditioned to believe they cannot break away. They believe the rope can still hold them, so they never try to break free."[4]

We're much the same way, aren't we? We've been trained through life circumstances and past sins we've committed and sins committed against us that we're enslaved to the way we are. We're conditioned to believe that we're "stuck." The reality is that God is bigger than those things, and He has begun a new work in us. We're free. Paul says in verse 11, *"Consider yourselves dead to sin and alive to God."* Paul uses the word *consider* because he wants us to start thinking in a new way. Behavior has a lot to do with our belief. Our behavior follows what we truly believe. If we believe that we are slaves to something, we will live enslaved. If we begin to believe the truth of the gospel and that God has empowered us to live for Him, it transforms how we behave.

I remember feeling trapped in my drug addiction for many years. When I first became a follower of Jesus, I used drugs the next day. For the first time in my life, I felt more than trapped. I also felt deeply convicted to change. I remember praying that day and begging God for deliverance from my habit. The next day when I awoke I was different. I really believe God healed me of a drug addiction that had enslaved me for more than half my life. I have never used drugs again. Part of this was the absolute transformation that God made in me which would be necessary for me to live through my current situation. The other part was that I was beginning to believe that God had empowered a new change in me and that I had the ability to

---

4. http://theunboundedspirit.com/short-story-the-elephant-and-the-rope/.

be different. My belief doesn't change reality, but it can change my behavior.

You see, we live trapped into mindsets. If the elephant in the example above knew it was big enough to break the rope, it would. We don't just need to change our behaviors, but to change our minds (*metanoia*). Here's another example about something that is just taken for granted in our culture today: cohabitation. Many today, both inside the church and out, believe that living together before marriage is a good idea. I once talked to a young woman who wanted to take some new steps in her faith but had already committed to moving in with her boyfriend. It was a tough conversation as I explained to her that God calls us to live separately and to live in sexual purity until we get married. Her family had recommended they live together before getting married, like her parents had. We were comparing what I believe with what she believed, much because of what her parents believed. Did you know that studies have determined that if you live together before marriage you are 33% more likely to get divorced than if you don't? And, did you know that it is just more than 50% of those who live together that actually get married? Would having the facts actually change your mind?[5]

If we believed the data that people who live together have a lower chance of getting married and staying married, would it change how we live? If you were in love with someone, you'd do everything you could to make it work. If I knew something was going to take the life out of a relationship, I wouldn't do it. I didn't think I'd be a drug-addicted person that wound up in

---

5. http://brandongaille.com/43-statistics-on-cohabitation-before-marriage/.

prison. I started out believing drugs wouldn't hurt anything. Those who have been addicted know this well. Drug use may have started out as a fun experience, but it didn't end well. If I had believed with all of my heart that the first time that I abused drugs or alcohol I'd wind up addicted, I would have never done it. Unfortunately, behavior follows belief.

Often in the church today we're given a set of rules of behavior (like not cohabiting, not doing drugs, etc.). But Paul is trying to help us see that a changed life isn't simply about trying to act differently. Paul spends his time on correcting our beliefs, not our behavior. When we learn to think and believe the truth of the gospel, we will live different lives. But if you don't believe it, you will continue to walk another way. In John 8:31 and 32, Jesus says, *"If you abide in my word, you are truly my disciples and you will know the truth and the truth will set you free."* This isn't merely the power of positive thinking; this is the reality of lives being changed by the power of the gospel applied to sinful people, setting them free.

Sin, Righteousness, and Two Dogs (Romans 6:12–16)

Let not sin therefore reign in your mortal body, to make you obey its passions. Do not present your members to sin as instruments for unrighteousness, but present yourselves to God as those who have been brought from death to life, and your members to God as instruments for righteousness. For sin will have no dominion over you, since you are not under law but under grace. What then? Are we to sin because we are not under law but under grace? By no means! Do you not know that if you present yourselves to anyone as obedient slaves, you are slaves of the one whom you obey, either of sin, which leads to death, or of obedience, which leads to righteousness?

Paul gives us some strong warnings about what we allow to reign in our lives. He posits that if we let sin reign, it will have more control; but if we don't, we will live like Jesus has called us to. Here is an example I heard a long time ago. I am not sure who originated it, and I have heard different versions. Here is one I like: the struggle between sin and obedience can be likened to two dogs that live inside you. One represents the sin and brokenness in our life, and the other represents our new life in Christ. These two dogs are at war with each other.[6] Yes, we've been crucified with Christ and given new life. But it's the dog that we feed that will win the battle. Let's bring the metaphors together: Paul basically says that whichever dog you feed will get stronger and be the victor over the other. You can be obedient to God or enslaved to sin. Those are our only options. Because Christ has set us free to serve God, we now have the ability to serve Him, and with that comes the responsibility to grow in obedience.

Because the gospel is true, because Jesus lived, died, rose, ascended, and reigns, and because we are empowered to live different lives, we ought not present ourselves to sin but to God as instruments of righteousness. When you belong to Jesus, the old self is put to death with Christ, and you're given a new self. God says that your sins have been removed. They were crucified with Christ and taken away. You've been forgiven, and you've been given new life. You're not defined by your sin any longer. You're no longer identified by your worst

---

6. http://tithenai.tumblr.com/post/17655980732/the-history-of-the-two-wolvestwo-dogs-story.

moments. In fact, you are identified by Christ's best moments. We're empowered to live new lives by grace.

God Replaces Hard Hearts with Hearts of Flesh (Romans 6:17–18)

> *But thanks be to God, that you who were once slaves of sin have become obedient from the heart to the standard of teaching to which you were committed, and, having been set free from sin, have become slaves of righteousness.*

Paul speaks to us now about how we are changed, and he talks about being *"obedient from the heart."* The metaphor changes from slavery to heart and back again, but the use of our hearts is deeply rooted in imagery that is used in the Bible. Here is one of my favorite passages in all of Scripture on this subject:

> *And I will give you a new heart, and a new spirit I will put within you. And I will remove the heart of stone from your flesh and give you a heart of flesh. And I will put my Spirit within you, and cause you to walk in my statutes and be careful to obey my rules.*
>
> *—Ezekiel 36:26–27*

In Ezekiel God promises to remove our hard heart (the heart of stone) and replace it with a heart of flesh. We're given a heart that can beat for God. The promise of a new life is so intertwined with the actual change of heart inside us that it reminds us that God can change every molecule in our body, that God can cause us to love new things and even lose the desires we have toward things that are not good for us. He promises to place His Spirit in us and causes us to walk in new ways. What a powerful promise about being able to make us brand new.

God is telling us that He's done all the hard work. But we still have a tendency to think our sin is our identity. The reality is that Jesus has opened the doors for us to walk in a different way because He's given us a different heart. But the fact still remains: we live our lives in tension between sin and obedience.

The Transparency of Paul (Romans 7:15-25)

How can we bring this full circle? How can we live faithfully in the tension that we're still not perfected human beings, and also live with authenticity of where we are right now? We'll skip ahead in Romans to chapter 7 where Paul gives us some deep insights on the subject:

For I do not understand my own actions. For I do not do what I want, but I do the very thing I hate. Now if I do what I do not want, I agree with the law, that it is good. So now it is no longer I who do it, but sin that dwells within me. For I know that nothing good dwells in me, that is, in my flesh. For I have the desire to do what is right, but not the ability to carry it out. For I do not do the good I want, but the evil I do not want is what I keep on doing. Now if I do what I do not want, it is no longer I who do it, but sin that dwells within me. So I find it to be a law that when I want to do right, evil lies close at hand. For I delight in the law of God, in my inner being, but I see in my members another law waging war against the law of my mind and making me captive to the law of sin that

105

*dwells in my members. Wretched man that I am! Who
will deliver me from this body of death? Thanks be to God
through Jesus Christ our Lord! So then, I myself serve the
law of God with my mind, but with my flesh I serve the
law of sin.*

What is going on here? The big idea is that Paul himself
continued to struggle deeply in his own life. Sin still existed
in Paul, for growth in holiness takes a long time. Paul could
see the difference between his flesh and the Spirit at work. The
war he was waging raged in his mind, yet had a spiritual reality
that was already completed. While his struggle was painful,
the outcome is good. God is ultimately the victor.

Keep in mind that this was Paul's struggle. Paul was a
high-level leader of the Jewish Pharisee group. Pharisees
were known as a people of the law. Paul's own life looked
put together as a devout Christian, a church planter, and a
pastor. But the reality was that he still struggled in life. He
wondered why he still chose the wrong thing sometimes. He
says, "There's sin still in me. It's not me; it's sin that lives in me."

Paul lived in-between. Does any of this sound familiar?
It should because it's the real-world experience of life as a
Christian day to day. If it was true of Paul, it's certainly true of
us too. We're all on a journey, walking on a path between who
we are and who we're called to be. We still fall short because
we're not perfect; sin is still in us. We still live in our broken
bodies and flawed world. But as we consider more what Christ
has accomplished for us and submit more to Him, we begin to
live new lives. Paul is very unfiltered when he says, "Listen, I
know the pain of living in the in-between. I know the pain of
the struggle. I still give in to sin, too." I wonder if the people

who knew Paul best ever thought to themselves, "Really? I didn't think Paul struggled like that."

What's different about Paul is that he was transparent and authentic about who he was and what he struggled with. He didn't put on a mask and pretend he was different. Hypocrisy is removed where there is an admission of failure, no pretense (a mask) of success. Transparency is admitting our brokenness while focusing on Christ's changes in us. Paul admitted that he still messed this up!

Living in the In-Between

We live in between the old self and the person Christ has called us to be. What do we do now? The Apostle Peter, one of the more prominent mistake-makers in the early church, gives us hope. He says this in Acts 2: *"Repent and be baptized every one of you in the name of Jesus Christ for the forgiveness of your sins, and you will receive the gift of the Holy Spirit."* Repentance is a change of mind that understands what Christ has done for you. Jesus said, *"You'll know the truth, and the truth will set you free"* (John 8:32). The problem in the Church is that when we call people to repent, we often call them to change their behavior. But people have belief problems, not behavior problems.

The impact of being immersed in Jesus is that we become honest with one another. Paul was honest. He didn't show up to church and pretend to have it all together. In his letters, he said, "Listen, I'm struggling and in pain here." There are times he wrote about his brokenness, imprisonment, struggle, pain, and trial. There are times he wrote about his joy in the same letter. We all know we can have that dichotomy in us. Not only was Paul honest enough to grow inside the community of faith, but he was honest enough to give the outside, on-looking world a glimpse of what it really means to follow Jesus. The world will know that we're followers of Jesus not by our pretending to have it all together, not by living with masks on like we're something that we're not, but rather by transparency and honesty. They'll know only when we portray ourselves as broken people living in between the cross and the resurrection.

Our Response

In light of this chapter, we're given a chance to respond in faith. First, we repent. We have a change of mind about who we are, what we've done, and the things we are enslaved to. As we come to those sober realizations, we turn from sin and turn to Jesus who "justifies" our account of sin to receive His righteousness. Second, we respond by getting baptized. If you are a new believer or have never been baptized, this is a way to receive a means of God's grace. We identify with Jesus's death and resurrection by going through the sacrament of baptism. Third, we are immersed in Jesus as we continually remember our baptism—that our sins were put to death with Him and that we were raised to new life. To stay immersed, we continue on with regular rhythms of the Christian life by doing things like going to church, hearing the Bible taught, and spending time with other Christians for regular encouragement and prayer. Fifth, we live a life of non-hypocrisy by taking off our masks, getting real with ourselves and with others, and living authentically—not like we have everything figured out. The Apostle Paul lived the life of authenticity, and we can too knowing that while we live a life in tension, Jesus has paid it all so that we can live free lives of love toward God and others.

CAN WE FIND REAL HOPE IN THIS LIFE?

Romans 8

We all endure pain and struggle. Sometimes our pain is temporary or situational. At other times we bear long-term or lifelong pain. How can we who follow Jesus find hope in this world and become better messengers of hope to others?

Christians are sometimes characterized in our culture as escapists—and sometimes rightfully so. On the one hand, there is at times a naïve assumption that if we were able to get back to a 1950s kind of world, everything would be perfect. Others believe elaborate end-times theories and are banking on Jesus coming back again any day to rapture them from their version of hell on earth. And sometimes Christians approach people in real need by giving bumper sticker solutions to troubles we all face in life, as if a problem can be solved in 140 characters or less: "God works all things together for good," "God loves the sinner but hates the sin," and "Someday there will be no more tears in heaven."

People mean well; they want to help, and give hope. But when people are dealing with real life problems, cheesy answers, Twitter-sized bits of wisdom, and escapist beliefs don't help. In fact, they often do damage. Often, pat answers minimize others' struggles and push people away from God rather than draw them in. When a loved one dies unexpectedly, when someone gets sick or divorce is looming, the last thing we need is for someone to give us a shallow attaboy.

Let's just admit it. We all struggle in this life. We all have pain. Sometimes it's short-term and situational. Other times we struggle for a lifetime. With that in mind, here are two questions I want to pose in this chapter: *how do we find hope, and how do we become better messengers of hope to others?*

Grounded, Real-Life Theology

The book of Romans is theologically oriented, but Christians don't always love the idea of theology. They think theology is for the seminary students who love to take Greek, Hebrew, and Latin courses. But theology simply means "Word of God" or "God's Word." A good explanation of the word *theology* is "understanding the Word of God in a cohesive way." When we begin to wrestle with tough questions of life, sometimes it's helpful to understand the big picture of Scripture and to do some theological exercises to better understand what God is saying to us today.

We Are in a Spiritual Battle (Romans 8:1–2)

There is therefore now no condemnation for those who are in Christ Jesus. For the law of the Spirit of life has set you free in Christ Jesus from the law of sin and death.

110

In the previous chapters, specifically what we covered in the "Why Am I So Broken" and "Are All Christians Hypocrites?" chapters, we're told there is a penalty for sin and that Jesus has paid that penalty. In this passage of Scripture, Paul transitions his theological argument by using the word *therefore*: he's saying that, because of what Christ has accomplished, God has not condemned us. We all endure suffering in this life, but it's not God punishing or condemning us for our sin or bad choices.

There's a difference between the general brokenness of the world and brokenness brought on by our individual sins. Jesus in John 9 addressed this very thing. That passage tells of a man blind from birth, and the disciples asked if the man was blind because of sins that he or his family had committed. Jesus's answer was that it was neither. The implications of a direct relationship between our sin and the struggles we have in life are important, but the other thing that we can take from this is that sometimes life just has issues. Our struggles and pain are not always something we have caused; they just might be because we live in a world that is broken.

As we have already unfolded, general brokenness is due to Adamic sin, but there is brokenness and pain due to the poor choices we make as well, and the pain that we cause due to our sin. There is cause and effect. Therefore, you may end up paying the penalty for those decisions. If you commit a crime, God will forgive you, but you might go to jail. As I've shared throughout this book, I had a long drug history in the 80s and the 90s. Though I quit in the 90s, there are still after-effects of my poor decisions. A good example is my physical health. Though I am fairly healthy, there is a residual affect on me because of the years of drugs, smoking, and unhealthy living that is part of that lifestyle. I have had a lot of dental work to repair teeth, which is common for someone who used the type of drugs I used. I've been forgiven by God, but there have been natural consequences for my sin. Those repercussions are not God's judgment, condemnation, or punishment; they are natural and physical consequences to the life I chose to live.

For those who are followers of Jesus, here's the truth: no matter what sins you have committed, if you have given your life over to Jesus, there is "no condemnation" for you (Romans 8:1). There are often natural consequences, but the spiritual and eternal consequences have been paid.

The image that best describes what Paul is saying here and what is developed later in this chapter is the image of a spiritual war. While it's true that there is no condemnation for us, we are still in a spiritual battle. Paul says that "the law of the Spirit" has set us free from "the law of sin and death." Though the eternal penalty has been satisfied, we are caught in the middle of a war and the battle-ground is our lives. The fight is between spirit and flesh. The war is real. We struggle, and sometimes we lose hope. Sometimes fatigue sets in, all because we are in a war. Feeling that we are broken and in pain can actually be a part of the spiritual battle we are in. Let's unfold this a bit in the upcoming verses.

Christ Is Victorious (Romans 8:3–5)

For God has done what the law, weakened by the flesh, could not do. By sending his own Son in the likeness of sinful flesh and for sin, he condemned sin in the flesh, in order that the righteous requirement of the law might be fulfilled in us, who walk not according to the flesh but according to the Spirit. For those who live according to the flesh set their minds on the things of the flesh, but those who live according to the Spirit set their minds on the things of the Spirit.

Paul states that what God has done overcame what we could not do by obeying the law. Because sin entered human history, our keeping the law is compromised. The law only exists to point out our need for a Savior.

In response to this, Jesus physically entered human history, becoming human (or as Paul says it, *"in the likeness of sinful flesh"*). Jesus came to fulfill the law by keeping it perfectly in our place. By accomplishing this, Jesus became victorious over sin. Don't miss this point because this is important: Jesus overcame what we have battled and lost, and He is victorious. We battle in this life, in our own power, and we lose. But Jesus comes in the power of the Spirit and has victory.

That brings us to the theological concept that I want to unpack in this chapter. *Christus Victor* is Christ's accomplishment and victory in the war of divine conflict. Many over the last 2000 years have defined this with different nuances, but when it is said that Jesus has overcome (had victory over) Satan, sin, and death, it means that Jesus has been victorious over the things that plague this sinful and broken humanity. Jesus has overcome the captivity of human struggle and pain by remaining sinless in His flesh, dying as a perfect sacrifice in our place, and defeating death in the resurrection. And He applies this "overcoming power" to us through the resurrection.

In a theological nutshell, *Christus Victor* is a Latin phrase that translates, "Christ is victorious." This means three things: 1.) Jesus has overcome the captivity of human struggle and pain by remaining sinless in His flesh. 2.) He endured the eternal penalty of sin by His death, and 3.) He has set us free from all that holds us captive in this life by His resurrection. Jesus applies this overcoming power to us through the Holy Spirit, in this life as well as for eternity. We live in the power of Christ's victories.

Paul writes in a letter to a different church that Jesus *"disarmed the rulers and authorities and put them to open shame, by triumphing over them"* (Colossians 2:15). It is in this triumph (victory) that Jesus empowers us to live. Paul will actually give us some practical steps in the next few verses.

When I first came to follow Jesus, I knew that I had to focus on something new and believe that Jesus was making changes inside me. I wouldn't have said the words *Christus Victor* at that time, but without knowing the theological reasons, or even practically how it was happening, I began to see the victory in my life. I was healed of a drug addiction, literally over night. Amazing. Something inside me was different, and I was hopeful.

Here is what Paul is saying: you can choose to focus on the struggles in your life, or you can begin to set your mind on the victorious power of Jesus in your life, and see what He does in you. Throughout the remainder of this chapter, we will unpack some real life applications based on what Paul unpacks for us.

Where You Set Your Mind Is Everything (Romans 8:6-8)

For to set the mind on the flesh is death, but to set the mind on the Spirit is life and peace. For the mind that is set on the flesh is hostile to God, for it does not submit to God's law; indeed, it cannot. Those who are in the flesh cannot please God.

Remember how we have already said in a previous chapter that we don't have behavior problems, we have belief problems? When it comes to hope, it's not a behavior problem. It's not a circumstance problem. It's where our mind is. Where you fix your mind is everything, according to the author of Romans. One psalmist writes about the same concept but uses a different phrase.

Psalm 119:15-16 says, *"I will meditate on your precepts and fix my eyes on your ways. I will delight in your statutes; I will not forget your word."* This is what happened to me in prison. I fixed my eyes (or set my mind) on something other than my present circumstance. No matter where you are today, no matter what your life looks like, no matter what your struggle is, where you set your mind is everything. If your mind is on present, difficult circumstances, it's easy to fall into hopelessness. I've spent lots of time feeling this way. And yet, when Jesus met me, He gave me a new focus. He focused my eyes on Him, and everything began to change.

When we fix our minds on the flesh (v. 7), we can't please God, and we become trapped in hopelessness. When our minds get trapped in our circumstances, our lives become trapped too. We act based on our situation, which results in even more hopelessness. This vicious cycle when our minds are "set on the flesh" causes a spiral of hopelessness that pulls us away from God in the very times when we need to draw near to God.

Application #1

In Christ we have a choice for how to view our struggles and pain: either through our current circumstances and limitations (flesh), or through what Jesus has accomplished for us (Spirit).

We Have Hope in Jesus (Romans 8:9–10)

You, however, are not in the flesh but in the Spirit, if in fact the Spirit of God dwells in you. Anyone who does not have the Spirit of Christ does not belong to him. But if Christ is in you, although the body is dead because of sin, the Spirit is life because of righteousness.

When you're going through something difficult, sometimes talk of hope can sound shallow. But please don't take this as an Oprah-ized mind-over-matter, think-good-thoughts kind of thing. There's no magical cure for getting through difficult times. However, there is true hope we can cling to. Our hope is about taking what Jesus has already given us and learning how to live it out.

If we were poor and homeless, and someone put enough money in our hands to give us a new life, we could still choose to continue to live as if we were poor, homeless, and hungry. But we're not poor and homeless. We have a wealth of hope, transformation, and life waiting for us. Jesus has already done it. We are no longer in the flesh (v. 9); therefore, Christians are invited to get on board with what stands between them and the victory Christ has already won. And this victory is given to us as an inheritance of Christ's righteousness (v. 10). We have hope because we have a guarantee of victory in Christ Jesus.

Application #2

We have hope because we inherit Christ's righteousness (victory over sin). When our sin is what causes us pain, we have a guarantee of victory in Christ and the empowerment to move into that victory.

Hope in Christ's Spirit (Romans 8:11)

If the Spirit of him who raised Jesus from the dead dwells in you, he who raised Christ Jesus from the dead will also give life to your mortal bodies through his Spirit who dwells in you.

This passage can be deeply meaningful for those going through deep ongoing issues in life. For over fourteen years, my wife has had chronic health problems; for twelve of those years, she's been completely bed-ridden. There have been times of hopelessness. During that time, I've never doubted God was good. I never doubted God *could* heal her. But, to be honest, I have struggled in prayer at times. When you pray the same thing over and over for years, you can get to a place of thinking, "God, I still believe you're good, but I'm simply out of words to pray." Christ's Spirit in me meets me in those broken, hopeless moments, and began to give me words again.

We have hope because Christ's Spirit lives in us. We have

hope for healing and hope when healing doesn't come quickly. Our hope and our strength exist because of His presence in us; it's not based on an outcome. My hope doesn't come from whether Lisa is in pain today or not. My hope comes because Christ's Spirit is in me and in Lisa regardless.

Now let's flip this idea over to Lisa's experience and imagine you're her. Imagine you're in bed and in pain. Maybe you have had chronic illness, and you already understand this. Hope doesn't come from the moments without pain. Because when the pain comes back, it's devastating. Our hope comes from Christ in us, from that inside peace where God shows up and meets us in the worst struggles, in our pain, suffering, and trials. Hope comes from knowing that this is temporary, even if it is seemingly endless, and that there is victory in Christ awaiting us.

Application #3

We have hope because Christ's Spirit lives in us. We have hope for healing, and hope when healing doesn't come quickly. Our hope and strength exist because of His presence in us, not because of an outcome.

Hope in Transformation (Romans 8:12–13)

So then, brothers, we are debtors, not to the flesh, to live according to the flesh. For if you live according to the flesh you will die, but if by the Spirit you put to death the deeds of the body, you will live.

We talked a little bit about this one, but here's where Paul is giving us hope for transformation. We have hope in Christ's victory over sin as we see changes take place in us that are beyond our own ability. Hope grows with each change and gives more hope for the future.

In the summer of 2015, I took the summer off for a sabbatical to write my autobiography. One of the things a publisher always asks is, "Why you, and why your book? Why not the million others that have a story like yours?" I sat down and asked myself, "Why my story?" There are a bunch of people that have been in prison and found faith.

Here's why I started writing, and here's what I wrote to the publisher that they found compelling enough to say yes to my writing a book. I've experienced more life change in my life than anybody I know. I have found hope, life, and a ton of transformation. It's not because of anything that I did, but it is entirely God who did something. Because of this, I can tell you that change is real, and hope is offered in Christ. I am not the person that I was twenty years ago. I remember the "old" me vividly. That guy had no hope and no power to change. God met me, changed me, and gave me hope that I'd never had before. Sometimes you have to stand on the stories of others. You have to hear the stories of life change in other people to get that hope that your life can change too. Maybe my story can be an encouragement to you while you wait for change in your own life story. When your life changes, let your story be an encouragement to others too.

Application #4

We have hope in Christ's victory over sin as we see changes take place in us that are beyond our own ability. Hope grows with each change and gives more hope for the future.

Our Hope in Adoption (Romans 8:14–17)

*For all who are led by the Spirit of God are sons of God.
For you did not receive the spirit of slavery to fall back
into fear, but you have received the Spirit of adoption as
sons, by whom we cry, "Abba! Father!" The spirit himself
bears witness with our spirit that we are children of God.
If children, then heirs, heirs of God and fellow heirs with
Christ, provided we suffer with him in order that we may
also be glorified with him.*

Abba is a Hebrew word that means "daddy." Let me ask you
this. If you stepped in to adopt an abandoned child, does that
child now have a new identity and a new family? Absolutely.
They may have wounds of abandonment, but they really are
part of a new family. We also live in the tension of having a
new identity, family, and home, yet we still struggle with
the pain of the past. But we have hope as adopted children
of God who are given an inheritance beyond measure. This
results in a completely new identity, one that calls the Creator
of the universe "Daddy." We're adopted into a place where
everything is different.

However, just because we're part of a new family doesn't
mean we won't experience struggle. Living this life in Christ
does not mean it's easy, as if everything in life is going to start
going right for you. When you give your life to Jesus, you
engage in a spiritual war. Though Christ is victorious in that
war, you still enter into a battle. In that battle, the battleground
is you, and it's a guaranteed struggle. But it's also a guarantee
of victory.

Our Hope Eternal (Romans 8:18)

For I consider the sufferings of this present time are not worth comparing with the glory that is to be revealed to us.

I don't want this verse to come off as one of those Twitter kinds of platitudes we spoke about earlier. But built on the foundation of the victories that Christ has won for us, this verse becomes incredibly powerful. Your eternity is secured. It's not in question. It's not something you can mess up. If God has rescued you, saved you, healed you, and adopted you, you belong to Him. Your future is secure. Hope is knowing the entire eternal and unending future is secure and in the hands of God. Jesus has secured that as the victor over Satan, sin, and death. Jesus says in John 10 that He holds you in His hand and no one can steal you away from Him. That means you can't steal you out, and someone else can't steal you out. You are secure in His hand. Does that mean you'll never make stupid decisions? No, not according to my life, at least. Does that mean you won't be without struggle? No, not at all. It just means if Christ is in you, the end is secure.

Revelation 21:4 says, *"He will wipe away every tear from their eyes. Death shall be no more. Neither shall there be mourning, nor crying, nor pain anymore, for the former things have passed away."* This is a glimpse and a promise Jesus invites us into. This is our future hope.

You see, hope isn't simply wishful thinking. We place our hope not in a positive outcome, but in the object of our hope, Jesus Himself. Jesus is the one who is victorious over sin and death, and He is making all things new. Even when you feel hopeless, remember, Jesus Himself is your hope. He was victorious so you could have hope.

Offer Hope to Others

Up to this point, this chapter has been about how you can find hope in this life. But how can we be a light to others who are in dark places? Here are two takeaways that you can use to help encourage others with the hope that you have:

1. Offer the hope Jesus gives here on earth to someone who is suffering today, not just the future hope of Heaven. The hope of heaven is great. But when someone is struggling today, they need immediate hope. Offer hope and love to people with real problems by fixing their eyes on Jesus and what He has accomplished for them.

2. Offer hope and love by listening, rather than giving simple answers to people with tough problems. Solutions don't come on bumper stickers or heal people in 140 characters. We all want to help, but sometimes listening and pointing people to Jesus is the best thing we can do.

IS IT ALL ABOUT
THE DOS AND DON'TS?

Romans 10

*If I obey the right "dos" and I avoid the appropriate
"don'ts," does that make me a good Christian? Is this what
Christianity really teaches?*

In my youth I was exposed to a very rules-based
Christianity. The problem was, I am not by nature a rule-
keeper. In response, I disobeyed the rules and got in lots
of trouble. To me, obeying the rules and Christianity went
hand-in-hand. I always understood Christianity as primarily
doing the right things and not doing the wrong things. I knew
Christianity proclaimed forgiveness, but it seemed to me that
post-conversion it became all about the *dos* and *don'ts*.

I remember saying as a teenager that I believed in Jesus
and the gospel, but I wasn't done having fun yet. In my
mind, the *dos* and *don'ts* of Christianity didn't look like an
enjoyable life. Now that I see Christianity much differently, I
am overwhelmed at how many people in the church approach

it as a system of *dos* and *don'ts*, of checks and balances that weigh out whether you are a good Christian or not. I wonder how many people outside the Church see Christianity as a system of rules and are turned off by it? Is this really what the Bible teaches?

Passionately Wrong (Romans 10:1–2)

Brothers, my heart's desire and prayer to God for them is that they may be saved. For I bear them witness that they have a zeal for God, but not according to knowledge.

Here is a quick look at the audience Paul is writing to. Paul addresses brothers, referring to a plural group of all the men and women readers; but the pronouns *them* and *they* refer to the Judaizers (the religious authorities we have spoken about in prior chapters). The Judaizers were corrupting Christianity by adding in all the Jewish rules and practices they believed in, as they attempted to combine Judaism and Christianity. They believed that to be a good Christian, you first had to be a good Jew, which meant obedience to the rules of Judaism. Much of what Paul writes in Romans is meant to address the Christians in Rome to clarify the expectations on them as followers of Jesus. Secondarily, Paul hopes the Judaizers who misled them will understand the true gospel and change as well.

Paul says that the Judaizers are zealous in their faith, but their zeal is *"not according to knowledge."* In other words, they are passionate, but they are passionately wrong. Paul understands what it's like to be religious and zealous for God and not know Jesus. At one time Paul was a religious leader who rejected Jesus and even persecuted Christianity. He had overseen the deaths of martyrs like Stephen who died in Acts 7.

He had a passion for following God, but he had rejected Jesus. A question we have to ask ourselves is, "Can we be passionate about God and simultaneously misunderstand what God wants from us?" Paul says yes. Likewise, the Judaizers have much zeal for God but are also very wrong.

Ignorance Offers Us Opportunity to Learn (Romans 10:3)

For, being ignorant of the righteousness of God, and seeking to establish their own, they did not submit to God's righteousness.

Ignorance is often heard as an offensive, condescending word. These days most people don't appreciate being called ignorant. In this case though, *ignorance* simply means lack of learning. I myself am ignorant of many things. I've never studied rocket propulsion, astrophysics, or trigonometry (and I'm capable of ruining a spreadsheet faster than anyone you know). To think of it this way is more relatable. We are all ignorant of certain subjects. We all are capable of gaining knowledge, but when we haven't studied something, we remain ignorant of it. When we are ignorant of something, we have an opportunity to learn something new and beneficial.

Paul says the people teaching the Christians in Rome are unlearned in their Jewish approach to the Christian faith. They're missing all that God has accomplished for them in Jesus. They teach Jewish Law (*dos* and *don't*s of Judaism), but they haven't yet learned what God has already done for them in Christ.

We too can lack understanding in our own faith at times. In our own passion, we attempt to pursue God in wrong ways.

That lack of understanding isn't wicked, but it is ignorant. To put it into more of a modern context, when I was younger, I was around well-intentioned people who wanted to please God with their approach to Christianity. They were passionate about Jesus, but it seemed as though they understood their faith best by the list of *dos* and *don'ts*. Were they passionate? Yes. They were also wrong.

Jesus the "End of the Law" (Romans 10:4)

> *For Christ is the end of the law for righteousness to everyone who believes.*

Christ is much more than a name. The Greek term for *Christ* is "Christos" (Hebrew version is "Messiah") and is defined as "the Anointed One," the one who fulfills all of God's promises. This Jesus, who is the Christ, is the redemption and reconciliation promised to us by God. Jesus is *"the end of the law for righteousness for everyone who believes."*

Before we go any further, we don't want to misunderstand the phrase *"the end of the law."* Throughout our study, the theme of righteousness has appeared often—righteousness meaning "morally justified or right before God." Elsewhere in Galatians 3:24, Paul says the purpose of the law is to act as a guardian to get us to Jesus. The law is not the end game of our faith; it is the means God uses to get us to understand our need for Jesus. When we measure ourselves by God's Law, we see that we continually fall short. It's then that we recognize our desperate need for Jesus, and we turn to Him in faith for forgiveness and reconciliation. We are justified and made righteous in the sight of God by faith in Jesus alone. Not through our obedience to the *dos* and *don'ts*. Put another way, let's define *righteousness* in the form of a question. How do we stand righteous before God without the overwhelming guilt of all our sin? Are we made righteous through rule keeping, or is it by Christ satisfying the rules in Himself? Jesus satisfied the law in his perfect obedience to the law. Therefore, Jesus is the *"end of the law"* for all who will believe in Him.

Jesus Advanced the Plot Line (Romans 10:5-7)

For Moses writes about the righteousness that is based on the law, that the person who does the commandments shall live by them. But the righteousness based on faith says, "Do not say in your heart, 'Who will ascend into heaven?' " (that is, to bring Christ down) or "Who will descend into the abyss?" (that is, to bring Christ up from the dead).

Moses wrote the first five books of the Bible, which contained the Jewish Law. It contains the Ten Commandments, rules for worship, celebration, and sacrifice to God. It also includes both civil and ecclesiastical laws. Paul is noting that Moses wrote about obedience to the laws of God and that Jesus came and fulfilled all of them. This may seem contradictory, but it's not. Here's an example of what I mean. Most of us are familiar with the main characters of the *Star Wars* movies. We know that Anakin is good and Vader is bad. This is not a contradiction; it just means that something happened to Anakin that turned him bad. Something big happened within the storyline that revealed the true arc of the story. If you were to only watch certain episodes of the many *Star Wars* movies without this understanding, you would remain "ignorant" of the plot line.

Likewise, those who learned about God before Jesus came

127

had a deep connection to the law. According to the law, the sacrificial system served as a way to cover their shortcomings in keeping the law. The good news is that Jesus has come and advanced the story and brought us the good news of the gospel. He has kept all the law perfectly in our place. Now, Jesus has come and fulfilled the law and is the righteousness of God. We are no longer tied to the Jewish Law, because Jesus fulfilled it. This doesn't mean we don't have boundaries to live by; it just means we can't please God by keeping the rules. Jesus has pleased God on our behalf.

Trying to Take Jesus's Place

Paul also gives us a challenge. Thinking we can obey the rules so well that our righteousness is based on our own efforts shows that we have a high view of ourselves. We don't ascend to heaven through our obedient actions. When we believe this, we're making a statement about Jesus. If we believe we're so good to stand before God on our own merit, then what is so great about what Jesus did for us? This would be the equivalent of bringing Christ down to our level. If our conception of faith is that we are capable of taking Jesus's place, then we would not need a Savior and the word *gospel* is meaningless.

What Does Scripture Say? (Romans 10:8-9)

> *But what does it say? "The word is near you, in your mouth and in your heart" (that is, the word of faith that we proclaim); because, if you confess with your mouth that Jesus is Lord and believe in your heart that God raised him from the dead, you will be saved.*

Is It All About the Dos and Don'ts?

I love this section of Scripture because it gets at the heart of one thing I hope to accomplish in this book. Whenever we engage tough questions of faith and struggle in our lives, my hope is that our desire is to ask ourselves, "What does the Bible say?"

Fortunately, God has spoken, and the answers are easy to find. The answers are in your mouth and in your heart. You know the answer because it is the foundation of your faith. If you are a follower of Jesus, it begins with a confession that you are broken, sinful, and in need of a Savior. That means that you, me, and everyone else on the planet cannot do it on our own. We can't merit righteousness, and we aren't good enough to justify ourselves. No one can stand before God based on his or her own obedience and holiness.

The good news is that you don't have to! Paul continues, *"Because, if you confess with your mouth that Jesus is Lord and believe in your heart that God raised him from the dead, you will be saved."* You can't stand on your own merit, and you don't have to. Jesus will gladly stand in front of you so that you are seen as righteous, justified, and holy. That is why the gospel is called good news.

This is the verse that we brought up in an early chapter of this book that asked what is required to be a follower of Jesus. Paul is writing this verse to address what our role is in our own salvation. Do we have to obey rules? Do we stop doing one thing and start doing another? Paul's answer is clear: "Confess with your mouth and believe in your heart and you will be saved." Your salvation is based on faith. You stand in Jesus alone.

Let's not lose sight of to whom, and why, Paul is writing. He's writing about the Judaizers who were requiring the new Roman Christians to live according to the Jewish law in order to be good Christians. But it's not about the rules; it's about placing your faith in Christ. It's about believing that Jesus lived the perfect life, died for your sins, and rose from the dead for you. Jesus is alive today. He not only rescues us, but He points us toward how to live and please God.

How do we live in light of these verses? We come to an understanding that we can't fulfill the rules. We can say along with Paul (Romans 7) that we don't do the right things. We confess it. We don't point to our rule keeping (we haven't kept the rules); we point to Jesus and align our lives to match our confession of faith. Our lives aren't perfect, but we're people aimed at Jesus.

Connecting Being "Saved" with "Righteousness" (Romans 10:10–13)

For with the heart one believes and is justified, and with the mouth one confesses and is saved. For the Scripture says, "Everyone who believes in him will not be put to shame." For there is no distinction between Jew and Greek; for the same Lord is Lord of all, bestowing his riches on all who call on him. For "everyone who calls on the name of the Lord will be saved."

When Paul uses the term *saved*, he uses it in relation to righteousness. As previously stated, righteousness is that perfect life before God in which everything we do is morally right, justifiable, and brings God glory. But we all know that none of us is righteous in and of ourselves. How do we deal with that? Paul uses the term *saved* because he knows we're saved *from* something—that is, the wrath of God (see Romans 3). Now, how are we to be righteous? It's the same for both

Jews and Greeks. That means the answer is the same for those raised to worship God according to Jewish customs and those who were not. They all are made righteous, and they are saved through Jesus Christ. Jesus is the only way to be rescued from God's wrath and to receive His riches.

If You Believe, How Can You Stay Quiet? (Romans 10:14–17)

How then will they call on him in whom they have not believed? And how are they to believe in him of whom they have never heard? And how are they to hear without someone preaching? And how are they to preach unless they are sent? As it is written, "How beautiful are the feet of those who preach the good news!" But they have not all obeyed the gospel. For Isaiah says, "Lord, who has believed what he has heard from us?" So faith comes from hearing, and hearing through the word of Christ.

If your brokenness is being put back together by God, it is not only your privilege to share your faith with others, but it is your responsibility. This doesn't mean that we fall back into the habits of a rules-based form of Christianity. Sharing your faith doesn't merit God's love. Sharing the gospel with others is a natural outpouring of falling in love with Jesus. When we love something—or someone—we can't help but talk about it. I'm a Mac guy (not a PC guy), I am a proud owner of two Jeeps, and I really enjoy In-N-Out. It's not hard to get me to talk about the things that I love. If this is true of trivial things like burgers, cars, and computers, why would I not also speak about Jesus? When I will gladly tell you about my love for my wife, why would I not be anything but glad to tell you about my love for Jesus?

Applying What We've Learned

If I obey the right "dos" and I avoid the appropriate "don'ts," does that make me a good Christian? Is this what Christianity really teaches?

Ultimately, it doesn't matter if you were raised in a structured religious family with lots of rules or not. It matters what you believe about Jesus today and how that transforms your life. For me, I was exposed to Christianity since grade school, but all I could see was a rules-based system that I wanted to run away from. Paul writes similarly about himself in some of his writings, but he took the opposite approach. He was more zealous about Judaism than anyone else. Though he had a passion and a zeal for God, he completely missed Jesus. He was living a life of obeying the rules, believing that at the end of his life he would stand before God morally justified, righteous, and acceptable. Put in modern terms, Paul thought that when he stood before God at the end of his life, God would look at him and say, "You're a good person. Come on in." Paul says that kind of understanding about our relationship to God is fundamentally missing the point of the gospel. Instead, God has always promised that He would enter into human history and do what only He can do: make us righteous and bring us to salvation in Jesus alone.

How do we live in light of all this? We know on the one hand that we don't receive God's love because of our obedience. We also know that we live with the reality of sin in our lives. Just because we already have God's full love and promise of redemption does not mean we're free to continue to sin either. Not only does obedience flow out of our love for God, but He also empowers us to live in a new way by giving us the Holy Spirit.

Consider Paul's example about sharing your faith with others. We should be so in love with Jesus that it's natural for us to talk about Him. We don't do this to earn our salvation, and it's not as though we lose our salvation if we fail to do so. Sharing our faith isn't a rule we have to keep; instead, it's the natural outpouring of loving Jesus.

This reminds me of a great image Matt Chandler once gave in a sermon: when a child learns to walk, the parents can't help but be excited about it. They make sure to let all their friends and family members know. No parent shows disgust with their kid if they fall down after a few steps. Instead, the parents are overjoyed and cheering their kid on. When you feel defeated in your spiritual walk, know that Jesus has done it all. You don't have to perform for God. Instead, you are now free to start walking in your faith. Yes, you will make some missteps and fall. But you can get up with confidence again knowing that your Father delights in you because of all that Jesus has done.

SHOULD CHRISTIANS SUBMIT TO LEADERS THEY DISAGREE WITH?

Romans 13

When Christians disagree with those in authority, what is a biblical response?

Three years ago, our church sold our building, and we moved to a school in the community. A local pastor who had rented that school in the past invited me out to lunch. He shared with me that some of the neighbors were unhappy on Sundays when church members parked in front of their houses. So he encouraged his church to not park in the neighborhood and gave them maps where they could park without disturbing the neighbors. He was a good witness by reaching out to the community. Our church followed suit, and we've had a similar outcome. People came to visit on Sundays, and some of them have come to faith.

We were well within our rights to park in the neighborhood as we pleased. But that wasn't the point. We wanted to be good neighbors and keep an eye out for the interest of others. We weren't simply trying to obey the local laws; we were looking to be courteous to our neighbors, and that lent us credibility in the neighborhood.

Before we jump into answering our chapter question, let's take a look at some of the most famous rules ever given.

The Ten Commandments

You shall have no other gods before me.
You shall not make for yourself a carved image.
You shall not take the name of the Lord your God in vain.
Remember the Sabbath day, to keep it holy.
Honor your father and your mother.
You shall not murder.
You shall not commit adultery.
You shall not steal;
You shall not bear false witness against your neighbor.
You shall not covet.
                                                    —*Exodus 20*

Many of us know the 10 Commandments—or at least can name a couple. However, who gets to have authority in how these matters are kept? Who gets to say whether we're worshiping other gods? God has the authority. God alone gets to command us not to make graven images or use His name in a common way (because His name is holy).

When we get into commandments such as "children obey your parents," God delegates authority to the parents. In the commandments about theft and murder, God delegates to civil authorities. The point I'm trying to make is that God has delegated power to people in authority. As followers of Jesus, how do we live under authority when leaders are flawed? Christians are under the authority of God, and that authority includes being under established human authority. Our obedience also has gospel implications. When others see our faithfulness in obeying authorities, we gain credibility in God's mission. The world is watching, and if we are contentious people unconcerned with law abiding, we will have no credibility.

Submission and Obedience (Romans 13:1)

Let every person be subject to the governing authorities. For there is no authority except from God, and those that exist have been instituted by God.

As this is being written, we're in the first 100 days of Donald Trump's presidency. This is one of the most contentious political seasons I've ever experienced. There are Christians on both sides of this debate. Some are in support of Trump while others support the groups that say, "#notmypresident." What I'm about to say next applies to Christians only. The rest of the world is held to a different standard. To Christians, Paul says, "*Be subject to the governing authorities.*" That includes the civil human authorities like the president. We don't typically like the idea of submission and obedience because leaders are flawed. But we're told in Romans 13, "*There is no authority except from God.*"

That last part of that verse reminds us that God has delegated authority to others. It's been instituted by God, and, therefore, all people in authority not only have authority but are under the authority of God. That means everyone in authority, whether that's church authority, parental authority, civil authority, federal governing authority, global authority, or whatever—those authorities are accountable to God. This has three implications for us.

"Those [authorities] that exist have been instituted by God":

1. *All authority is derived from God.*

2. *All authority is accountable to God.*

3. *We are to be subject to authority because of our subjection to God.*

Are We Following God or Man? (Romans 13:2)

Therefore, whomever resists the authorities resists what God has appointed and those who resist will incur judgment.

Remember, our obedience to human authority is the outcome of our obedience to God.

Notice, there are no qualifications to the kinds of authority God is talking about in these verses. I know no matter what I write after this, someone will say there is an exception to this rule. The objection is understandable. If a father is abusing his daughter, clearly we are not talking about obeying that kind of abuse. If a fascist leader tells his citizens to execute innocent people, clearly we are not talking about that kind of abuse either. If anyone is in a situation in which he or she is being abused by an authority, that person should seek a trusted person in authority and talk about it.

Back to President Trump. You may have voted for or against him, but whatever your position, he won. What's your role?

Many will not like the answer, but it is to submit as a part of our obedience to God. Trump is accountable to God, and he will answer for his presidency. Our job is to hear the words of Paul and take them seriously. *"Whoever resists the authorities resists what God has appointed and those who resist will incur judgment."* But remember, the issues at hand are not outside God's control either. Our God is sovereign and bigger than any presidency or nation.

As Christians we are called to be obedient and subjected to authority because God delegates authority in this world. God doesn't say to obey your parents if they are good parents. He says to obey your parents. Parents, God says, must love their children—no matter how challenging they might be. Citizens, honor your leaders even if they are dishonorable.

Authority Is No Problem When You Obey (Romans 13:3-4)

For rulers are not a terror to good conduct, but to bad. Would you have no fear of the one who is in authority? Then do what is good, and you will receive his approval, for he is God's servant for your good. But if you do wrong, be afraid, for he does not bear the sword in vain. For he is the servant of God, an avenger who carries out God's wrath on the wrongdoer.

As followers of Jesus, we are to obey all established authority, not because the person or system itself is perfect, but because it is set in place by God for our collective good. But when it comes to civil authority, we often get afraid, don't we? Paul says that the *"rulers are not a terror to good conduct but to bad."*

Frustrated

Here's a funny, real-world example. When you see a cop, do you immediately hit the breaks? The Sunday that I originally preached this passage, I got on the freeway and took off at my normal pace—which is often above the speed limit. Having just written a message on this passage I was about to deliver, I thought to myself, "If I saw a cop right now, what would I do? I would immediately pump the brakes because I was going over the speed limit." I slowed down as I was thinking about it and looked over to my right and saw a motorcycle cop on the side of the road. I broke out laughing in my car. What would I have done if I hadn't slowed down? I would have definitely flinched and looked down to see how fast I was going. Paul says, *"Rulers are no terror to good conduct."* Is that cop on the side of the road a terror to good conduct? No. Should he have ticketed me three minutes earlier? Yes, he should have.

But then there are those folks who get a traffic ticket, and they feel angry at the cops. But that police officer has a job to do. This just shows how entitled our culture is. The media narrative right now is that a cop is wrong by default. If someone resists arrest and is hurt in the process, we often make a big deal about how aggressive the police get when really it may be an issue of disobedience. Now this isn't true for every example, but normally this is the case.

There is always room for dialog about wrongdoing among authorities. But should we not first ask ourselves how we should respond to authority? If we get in trouble, if we flinch when we see a cop parked on the side of the road, if we have that attack of conscience, it's probably because we are not doing the right thing.

Obedience As an Issue of Faith (Romans 13:5)

Therefore one must be in subjection, not only to avoid God's wrath but also for the sake of conscience.

We obey the laws for two reasons: to avoid God's wrath and to acknowledge our conscience. The issue of conscience is fairly simple. When I saw the cop on the side of the road, it was funny and my conscience was clear. What if we talked about our obedience in relationship to obeying God no matter how big or how small the infraction? Suddenly the conversation changes when my driving is a reflection of my relationship to God. When I obey the law because I'm obeying God, I reflect Christ to those around me (especially since I have a Generations Church sticker on the back of my jeep).

Bringing this back to the issue of a controversial president, it doesn't matter if your controversy is with Trump, Obama, or Bush. If we view our submission to a president that we disagree with as submission to God Himself, it changes the way we respond. I'm not suggesting that people shouldn't protest and march if they're in disagreement over policies; but as Christians, we are subject to governing authorities.

This is an issue of our worship, and it should change our political discourse and responses to things we may not agree with. We don't have to agree with any particular president to live as God has called us to. Our relationship with Jesus is reflected in the smallest point of our obedience and disobedience because it reveals our hearts. Bigger than that, it also reflects Christ to the community.

Seeing our obedience to governing authority as being obedient to God makes our disobedience about God as well. Picking and choosing which rules or leaders to obey is in reality placing ourselves in authority over God and whom He has allowed to be in leadership. When we do that, it's sin. Sin is missing the mark of holiness and worship. When I choose which traffic laws to obey, I'm saying that I know better than the God who put them in place.

Proverbs 18:12 says, *"Pride comes before a fall but humility before healing."* Our arrogance causes pain, but humility brings healing. Our arrogance of thinking we know better than everybody else comes at a cost. Humility embraces that rules are there for our own good and for the protection of the people around us. We have incredible opportunity as Americans. We can change laws we disagree with. But how we do this matters. It is a reflection of our worship.

Acceptable Disobedience, Paying Taxes (Romans 13:6)

For because of this you also pay taxes, for the authorities are ministers of God, attending to this very thing.

It is commonly known that we all hate to pay taxes. Every political season, politicians promise to do something about the issue of taxes, but don't follow through. Some people cheat on their taxes in different ways. Maybe they write off a meal as a business expense.

The problem is, again, we find ourselves picking and choosing which rules are acceptable to break.

Jesus addresses this when asked if it's lawful to pay taxes. Of course, the question is a trap because if Jesus says, "Yes, you should pay taxes," the people get mad. If He says, "No, you shouldn't pay taxes," the government is going to be mad. Ingeniously, Jesus asked them to show Him a coin and asked whose picture is on it. And of course it's Caesar's picture. Then he says, *"Give to Caesar the things that are Caesar's and give to God the things that are God's"* (Matthew 22:21). Do you see? If we give to God what is due to God, we're naturally going to pay our taxes because that is what the law says to do. Obedience to human authority is inextricably linked to our obedience to God. When asked about taxes, Jesus ties taxes to our relationship and obedience to God.

Give Everyone His or Her Due Respect (Romans 13:7)

Pay to all what is owed to them: taxes to whom taxes are owed, revenue to whom revenue is owed, respect to whom respect is owed, honor to whom honor is owed.

If you owe taxes, pay them. If you are an employer, pay your people. If you are in debt, pay your debtor. To those whom respect is due, like civil authorities, give them respect. To those who are due honor, like parents and leaders, give them honor. Even in this vitriolic political climate, God calls us to honor and respect all those in authority. We will never agree with every leader and decision, but we are called to treat each as God has commanded.

Jesus: Our Perfect Model

If Jesus owed taxes, do you think He would have paid them? If Jesus owed money to someone, would He have paid it? Did Jesus give respect and honor to people who were due it? When Jesus was arrested, falsely accused, and on trial for His life,

He gave respect to the authorities over Him. Looking back at the first century rulers, none of them were without deep corruption. Yet Jesus always acted respectfully.

Think about this. If Jesus were on social media, would He post the things that Christians post today about political candidates, law enforcement, or those He disagrees with? Social media has given rise to demeaning others we don't agree with. Does your social media profile say you are a Christian? Whom do you represent on Twitter, Facebook, and Instagram? Do you engage online with grace, honor, and respect? Do the jokes you forward on and the things you say represent Christ well? If we're honest with ourselves, our social media profiles often misrepresent our faith.

In the most recent election cycle, I was saddened by how Christians engaged on social media. The names they called candidates was distasteful. We're accountable for the disrespect we show to others.

Obedience Is Also about Loving Others (Romans 13:8–10)

> *Owe no one anything, except to love each other, for the one who loves another has fulfilled the law. For the commandments, "You shall not commit adultery, You shall not murder, You shall not steal, You shall not covet," and any other commandment, are summed up in this word: "You shall love your neighbor as yourself." Love does no wrong to a neighbor; therefore love is the fulfilling of the law.*

As Christians we have a debt of love to everyone because Christ first loved us. In fact, Christ loves us when we were at our most unlovable. Now that we have received God's love, we are called to be agents of that love to others. Jesus says that love fulfills all the commandments. If you're busy loving God, you're not going to have other gods. You're not going to take His name in a common way and demean Him. Jesus says that all the commandments hinge on loving God and loving your neighbor as yourself (Matthew 22:37–40). Do you see that when you are occupied with loving others, you simultaneously refrain from breaking God's laws? When you're busy loving someone, you're not going to murder them. If you're loving your neighbors as you love yourself, you won't steal from them. If you're busy loving your spouse, you're not going to love anyone else; faithfulness to your spouse follows naturally.

Do We Have Any Responsibilities Beyond Obedience?

Paul gives a challenge to a church in another letter about praying for people in authority. Here's what he says,

> "First of all, then, I urge that supplications, prayers, intercessions, and thanksgivings be made for all people, for kings and all who are in high positions, that we may lead a peaceful and quiet life, godly and dignified in every way. This is good, and it is pleasing in the sight of God our Savior, who desires all people to be saved and to come to the knowledge of the truth."
>
> —1 Timothy 2:1–4

Paul not only says to submit, obey, and give honor, but he also says to pray. As Christians, we should pray for our leaders.

As we pray, our hearts change, and we expect that God can change our leaders' hearts in any ways that are displeasing to Him. Paul says this is good and pleasing to God. Now he goes a step further and brings us back to the relationship between how we live and how our lives reflect Jesus to others. The way we live images Jesus to the world. Obedience and submission to those we disagree with should reflect our worship of God.

WHAT IS TOLERANCE AND WHAT IS JUDGMENT?

Romans 14

Both the Bible and the culture we live in have much to say about tolerance and judgment. How does the Bible help us reconcile these two things?

I n our political and cultural climate today, we hear the words *tolerance* and *judgment* a lot. Christians are said to be judgmental, and often that's true. Also those that proclaim tolerance the most are only open to their own views, not necessarily with folks who disagree with them. We all have this judgmental tendency. How do we wrestle with this as it relates to our faith?

Jesus on "Judgment"

Before we dive into the text from Romans, there are three verses about judgment to address. All are the very words of Jesus Himself. Notice that some of these verses command us to judge, while others prohibit it. We will define this in a minute.

"Judge not, that you be not judged" (Matthew 7:1).

"And why do you not judge for yourselves what is right" (Luke 12:57).

"Do not judge by appearances, but judge with right judgment" (John 7:24).

The culture around us says, "Don't judge me," but everyone makes judgments every day. We judge what is right and wrong, and we make judgments about others and how they live. How do we live in light of this reality? The biblical passages above talk about three different things. The command not to judge is about not judging eternally (Matthew 7:1). That is definitely not our job. However, we are called to make judgments, maybe better translated as *discernments* for clarity (Luke 12:57). Though these verses may seem contradictory, they have very different meanings. We are also given some warnings about not judging based on appearance (John 7:24). That same verse closes with *"judge with right judgment."* There must be a way for a Christian to judge faithfully according to the Word of God. With all that in mind, what does God say about tolerance? What does God say about judging? How can we live simultaneously faithful to God and loving to others who might be very different from us?

Serving Those "Weak in Faith" (Romans 14:1)

As for the one who is weak in faith, welcome him but do not quarrel over opinions.

What Is Tolerance and What Is Judgment?

There are some things we should consider here. First, what does it mean when someone *"is weak in faith"*? This is the person with an issue of conscience over something morally neutral. This could be someone new to the faith or someone who has been a believer for a long time. Someone may also be weak in faith due to a particular background or struggle. For example, if someone grows up around alcoholism, that person may be more sensitive to those who responsibly have a glass of wine at dinnertime. Some things are morally neutral; it just depends on how you do it.

Said another way, take a dollar bill out of your pocket and consider this: is that dollar bill morally negative or positive? It's neither. You could use that money to pay a thug to go hurt someone, or you could send money to a Third World country so that those people could have clean water. You could use that money for something evil or you could use it for good, but the dollar bill doesn't change. It is morally neutral. Often, when we hear that someone is weak in faith, we hear it condescendingly. It might be somebody newer to the faith or someone who hasn't found a particular freedom in the gospel yet. We should never assume we know someone's full story.

Paul says, *"As for the one who is weak in faith, welcome him, but not to quarrel over opinions"* (Romans 14:1). Our first challenge as followers of Jesus from this Scripture is not to argue with someone over an issue of conscience. You don't have to be right. Paul says to welcome such people. We are not to argue with them over their issue of conscience but to love them right where they are. We just spoke about someone who grew up with alcoholic parents. Let's not assume we know everybody's back story.

At Generations Church there are people who were atheists

and now follow Jesus. We have people who have come out of cults. There are people who have struggled with addiction, and people who have come from different streams of Christianity or different forms of church—some more traditional and some non-denominational backgrounds. All these inform and shape our convictions.

Dietary Rules of the Past (Romans 14:2–3)

One person believes he may eat anything, while the weak person eats only vegetables. Let not the one who eats despise the one who abstains, and let not the one who abstains pass judgment on the one who eats, for God has welcomed him.

In Romans, Paul writes about issues from his specific time and context. His first example isn't a controversy in the church today, so it's a great place for us to start.

In first century Christianity, there was a group of people in Rome who were similar to what might be called vegans today. They didn't eat meat, only vegetables, but they did it as a way of glorifying Jesus. We also have people like that today. Are these people morally right or wrong? Sometimes they claim their dietary convictions from Scripture; but for the most part, we know we don't need to change the point of view of the person who eats at McDonald's over to non-GMO and vegan food. We don't need to "fix" people with alternate points of view. Likewise, if someone else is newer in the faith or struggling with a particular issue, we don't need to be right. We are called to come together on issues that are either less clear or morally neutral.

Who Makes You the One to Judge? (Romans 14:4–6)

Who are you to pass judgment on the servant of another? It is before his own master that he stands or falls and he or she will be upheld for the Lord is able to make him stand. The one who observes the day, observes it in honor of the Lord. The one who eats, eats in honor of the Lord since he gives thanks while the one who abstains, abstains in honor of the Lord and gives thanks. One person esteems one day better than another, while another esteems all days alike. Each one should be fully convinced in his own mind.

It's a tough balance to find your way down the center of opposing issues, and for many of us it's because we were raised or taught one of these ways. Paul says, "Who are you to pass judgment on the servant of another?" In the case of people with convictions different from ours, how do we know that God hasn't given them that conviction for a specific purpose? Maybe it's baggage from their background, or maybe God wants to use their conviction to advance the gospel. So who are we to judge that conviction? God is able to see the Gospel take root and transform lives wherever that person is. It's tough to stay balanced on issues when we have strong opinions about things. Again, we're not talking about black and white issues, but things that are not outright forbidden. These could be issues of whether it's appropriate for a Christian to drink alcohol or not, or issues of diet. Not only are we called to not judge people of different convictions, but we're also called to live according to our own convictions.

Traditional versus Nontraditional

Paul's second example isn't really explosive in our context, but consider that some people come from a very traditional form of church while others come from a more casual form. Some folks that attend our church would prefer to wear a suit and a tie. Others prefer shorts and flip flops. Some like a high liturgical form of church. Some don't. A lot of that is shaped by how we're raised, where we met Jesus, and how those traditions are meaningful to us.

In Paul's day, there were people who were coming from Judaism to Christianity who were still upholding high feast days, but they were also demanding that new Roman and Greek Christians should observe these days too. Of course we all should live according to our convictions, we just shouldn't push secondary, non-gospel issues on other believers. In the case of these Jewish convictions, there is no reason for the non-Jewish Christian to observe them. However, for the Jews that found holiness in those traditions, it's OK for them to continue to practice them.

Be Convinced in Your Own Mind

There's a caution in here for us. Everyone should be convinced in his or her own mind. We live in a time with a lot of moral relativism. We live in a time when there's not a whole lot of absolute truth. However, life is full of absolutes. One plus one equals two all the time, every time whether it's true for you or not. A moral relativistic answer is not going to get you to pass a math class. If we run a red light and hurt someone else, it's our fault, whether we think the red light's right or wrong.

There are a lot of parameters and guardrails in life, but within those guard rails, Christianity is a far wider lane than we give it credit to be. Within that lane, Paul says if you choose to be vegan, be a vegan for Jesus. Have at it. If you choose to barbecue and eat meat, God bless you; do it for Jesus. You want to dress nice, dress nice. You want to wear shorts and flip flops, do it for Jesus. But don't judge the people who find their worship and their connection to Christ differently from how you do.

We Don't Live in Isolation but among the Body of Christ (Romans 14:7–9)

For none of us lives to himself and none of us dies to himself. For if we live we live to the Lord, and if we die we die to the Lord, so then whether we live or we die, we are the Lord's, for to this end, Christ died and lived again, that he might be both Lord of the dead and the Lord of the living.

Here's where Paul's argument shifts. He reminds us that this life isn't just all about us. Then he ties his idea to Jesus. He reminds us that we're not here for ourselves; we're here for others and for the glory of God. How we live in light of debatable or morally neutral convictions impacts others both inside and outside the church. Paul calls the more mature believer to sacrifice for the weaker brother, and he calls all believers as Jesus did toward outsiders. Jesus sacrificed for others, and we are being called to the same thing. That means that we live on the same mission Jesus was on. To love and serve others as He did.

Why Do We Pass Judgment? (Romans 14:10–12)

Why do you pass judgment on your brother? Or you, why do you despise your brother? For we will all stand before the judgment seat of God; for it is written, "As I live, says the Lord, every knee shall bow to me, and every tongue shall confess to God." So then each of us will give an account of himself to God.

Here Paul asks a powerful question: "Why do we pass judgment?" Could it be that our judgments of others are flawed either in our desire to be right or our desire to justify our own behavior? More often than not, when we want to be right, it's usually because of a selfish reason instead of wanting to love and serve the other person.

In verse 12 Paul says that we will all stand before God and give an account for our lives. Here's where we can really challenge ourselves. When we stand before God, what will He say about how we judged others? Were we filled with grace toward people with convictions different from our own? When we make a stand for something, was it because we wanted to love others and do what is right for them? Or do we just want to be right? For all these things we are accountable to God.

How Do We Live This Out?

Let's close this chapter a little differently. I want to give practical applications right out of the verses. Because the verses are clear, we will go over them again, and I'll give you a challenge from each verse.

What Is Tolerance and What Is Judgment?

Therefore let us not pass judgment on one another any longer, but rather decide never to put a stumbling block or hindrance in the way of a brother.

—*v. 13*

Stop passing judgment on others over matters of conscience and begin to live sacrificially. Just take one for the team. When you go to a home where they don't drink alcohol, then don't drink alcohol. You go to a home where they're vegans, eat a salad. Eat a salad for Jesus. Quit judging other Christians and start to live sacrificially so that others might see and grow in Christ.

I know and I am persuaded in the Lord Jesus that nothing is unclean in itself, but it is unclean for anyone who thinks it unclean.

—*v. 14*

If someone lives in the conviction that something is wrong, for that person to go against his or her conscience is sin. Come alongside them; don't try to fix them. If for them eating meat is wrong, then for them to eat a steak is wrong, because they would be violating their own conscience. Maybe God has placed this issue of conscience in them for a reason that's unknown to us. Maybe God has called them to be vegan so that they have an impact on another vegan's life. I don't know, and you don't know. But for them to live outside of their conviction would be sin.

If your brother is grieved by what you eat, you are no longer walking in love by what you eat. Do not destroy the one for whom Christ died.

—v. 15

If your freedom grieves someone else, love says *you* make the sacrifice instead of expecting *him* to. If you're with someone and disagree about an issue of conscience, you both should sacrifice in love for the other. If it's a morally neutral or debatable issue, who gives first? You give. Jesus sacrificed for us; we can sacrifice for others.

There are things that the Bible gives us freedom in, and there are things that the Bible is unclear about. That's OK. We have freedom in these areas. However, not everyone sees these freedoms the same way. Our challenge for tolerance is to love others who view these things differently. Our challenge for judgment is to discern right and wrong for ourselves and live by those convictions.

CONCLUSION

A s a pastor, I preach and teach often. I preach most Sundays at Generations Church, I've pastored several churches, and I've spoken at conferences, retreats, and many fun places. My favorite compliment from people who hear those messages is, "I've read [insert any book of the Bible] several times and heard it taught many times, but I've never heard it taught like that before." This isn't my favorite compliment because I want the praise—I don't care about that. Instead, I love this comment because it shows how simple teaching can be. I don't teach anything profound or earth-shattering.

I teach differently from most pastors though. I tackle larger passages each Sunday than most pastors do so that I can show the full context of the passage instead of pulling out isolated verses. The Bible wasn't written in verses to be separated and isolated—for example, the book of Romans was a letter intended to be read in a sitting. So, I teach through large chapters and passages aiming at the one main theme I see being unearthed, instead of trying to make many different points.

I also don't quote many authors or theologians, or even

use a lot of references. I just let the Bible do its job and try to stay out of the way. Understanding the Bible is simply about asking what God intended for a human author, like Paul, to write, so that the intended hearer, like the church in Rome, could understand. Now, 2,000 years later, we of course need to understand the cultural background, such as who the Judaizers were so we understand the context. But a good study Bible will teach this (I recommend the ESV Study Bible—you can purchase it on Amazon for around $25.00). Armed with a few contextual notes, the average Bible reader can learn much by approaching the Bible with an open perspective, instead of just inserting the opinions collected from everyone else.

If I Accomplished My Goal . . .

If I have accomplished my goal for this book, three things have happened. First, you have been pointed to Jesus. Jesus is God in human form—eternally God, though He became human so that you could see Him, know Him, and be transformed by Him. If you have seen Jesus in this book, that is a huge win for me. Second, I hope you have seen the Bible in a new way. The Bible is God's Word written to lead you into a transforming relationship with Him. God has superintended it so that it remains perfect in pointing us back to our Creator. God's Word is sufficient, and if I did my job, the pages of Romans have given you life. Last, if I have accomplished my goal, you don't think any higher of me, but only of Jesus. Without Jesus, I would still be in a prison cell or worse. I am nothing, and Jesus is everything.

When I set out to write this first book, my hopes were that I would reach an audience who had questions about what God says regarding faith and Christianity. I will quickly admit that Christianity has moved away from holding the Bible as authoritative and inerrant. Top that off with the fact that each generation of the church has struggles and failures, and the world now sees a flawed Christianity, but not the flawless Jesus and power of the gospel. This book is replete with my flaws and failures, both past and today. I struggle. I sin. I fail. A lot. But Jesus has never failed me, and He will never fail you. The Bible is true, authoritative, inerrant, and infallible. It is the source of life and truth for the follower of Jesus, and it reveals a God passionately in love with us, desiring to see humanity live the way we were intended to live.

If I get the chance to write again, I'll write about another book of the Bible. Apart from the Bible, I have nothing to offer you. My words don't give you life when you're dying inside. My words can't comfort you when you're in pain. I can't overcome your struggle, or change what afflicts you. What I can do is point you to Jesus and show you His Word. I am satisfied in Him. His Word is enough.

So, What Now?

I encourage you to find a church that teaches the Bible—not in disconnected, topical ways, but in ways that teach you how to read and understand the Bible for yourself. Let them walk you through whole books of the Bible, teaching you how to unearth God's truth for your life. When I finish teaching a book of the Bible, I want people to know what the actual book is about, instead of only remembering nuggets or sayings from a topical message. Each book of Scripture was written with a purpose, and that purpose has a place in our lives.

If you can't find a good church, get in touch with me.[7] I will answer.

I pray that you find a Bible-teaching church and that you grow in your faith.

Thank You!

Thank you for reading this. It is an honor and privilege for me to finally write and publish this book. May it point people to Jesus. He alone is worthy.

---

7. Twitter: @jeffludington, Facebook: facebook.com/jeffludington